C000253206

BECOME THE ROCK STAR RIGHT NOW!

Do you feel sick and tired of settling for less? Find out how to get clear and confidently step towards the rock star version of yourself in **Chapter Five**.

Do you feel like you have no control over what happens everyday? Turn to **Chapter Nine** to learn how to shift your mind and take charge.

Are you feeling unsure of yourself or a decision you're making? Turn to **Chapter Fifteen** to learn how to listen to your inner guidance.

Do you feel like you don't belong and are having trouble dealing with people in your life? Check out **Chapter Seventeen** to learn how to see the value in yourself and others.

Are you experiencing tons of stress and anxiety right now? Go to **Chapter Twenty-Six** for two of the most helpful techniques to relax and calm down.

YOU ARE THE
ROCK STAR

STEP INTO YOUR POWER AND LIVE YOUR
PURPOSE

ALEXANDER WOODROW

First printing, January 2020

ISBN-13: 978-1-7320220-1-0

Published by Granite Made

YOU ARE THE ROCK STAR

Copyright © 2020 by Alexander Woodrow. All rights reserved.

Author Photo by Louis Fisher. Copyright © 2020 by Alexander Woodrow. All rights reserved.

All material herein is presented "as is" with no warranty for any specific purpose, whether given or implied. Furthermore, this material is not intended to diagnose, prevent, treat, or cure any disease or condition. Always consult a professional before undertaking any of the advice herein to verify if it is safe for you. By reading this book, you understand that nothing herein is either expressed or implied to be legal, medical, or psychological advice, but only the author's opinion. Neither the author, nor his affiliates, heirs, partners, or publishers assume any responsibility for any errors, inaccuracies, omissions, or negative results when undertaking the advice herein.

All quotes, excerpts, and trademarks are used under "Fair Use" statutes for educational and review purposes. They remain the exclusive property of the respective copyright and/or trademark holders. No challenge to their ownership is given or implied.

Without limiting the rights under copyright above, no part of this book may be reproduced, stored in or introduced into a retrieval system or transmitted, in any form or by any means (electronic, mechanical, photocopying, recording, or otherwise), without the written consent of both the copyright holder and the above publisher of this book.

 Created with Vellum

Dedicated to my parents

Thank you for your patience while I pursued a career that "wasn't a career." Thank you for leading by example. Thank you for challenging me to be better, more informed and wise with my decisions. Thank you for being as proud of me as I am of you. And thank you for being the best role-models a kid could ask for... even when I didn't know it.

You are the real rock stars.

CONTENTS

FOREWORD

Wisdom books and ancient teachings all tell us the guru is inside. It's the truth for anyone who has ever experienced a moment of synchronicity, a connected feeling in meditation, or flow state during a really great run. The human experience tells us we have what we need inside, and we've all felt this in at least one moment in our life.

But often it's fleeting. It's almost too massive to take ownership, and it's so easy to give away our power to someone more charismatic, more achieved, more spiritual. It's so easy to fall into the trap of fear and anxiety and stay on the hamster wheel of endless comparison. It's so easy to buy loads of products that have a big feel-better promise, and leave us empty and more disconnected. We continue these destructive habits because even though we know the truth deep down, it feels impossible to find a better way.

The truth that Alexander "Woody" Woodrow reminds us of is simple and profound. You're the Rock Star. You have what you need inside. That is the starting point, the seed, your base. From here you can cultivate a process to nurture your individual power, talents, and capabilities to be well.

Good leaders, people using their full potential for good, are here to remind us, guide us, and pull us back on the path that we know is our own. Woody Woodrow is this kind of leader, and he really cares about you.

I met Woody several years ago in a Strala Yoga weekend training. He was an instant stand-out, and not just because his career is being an actual rock star. He is a spiritual warrior. His attitude is one of inclusion, dissolving negativity and empowering capability. He lives life's biggest secret: we rise not in isolation but together, by lifting up the people around us. Everyone for Woody is unique, special, and important. He is physically capable with yoga, and with everything, because he knows the truth. Your body can do what your mind believes. Woody wrote this book because he wants to share the truth with you. You are a rock star. We all are.

You Are the Rock Star shares the process of living in this truth, through the modern voice of someone in the music community, the healing community, and yoga community. The reality is we are all in one shared human community, and when we practice connecting with who we are, we remember we all are rock stars. Woody takes you through his journey and the essential process that will take you from where you are to where you would like to be. The best part, Woody reminds you how to enjoy every step of the way.

Let the party begin!

Tara Stiles
Founder of Strala Yoga

INTRODUCTION

I WROTE THIS BOOK for you, and I wrote it for me. I wrote it for everyone who wants to take control of their life to get what they want. It doesn't matter if your dream is to be a literal rock star, or an actor, an artist, an athlete, an author, an entrepreneur, etc. Whatever you want to be, you can be.

There is no trick; getting results takes effort. If you aren't willing to try, no book can help. But I promise, if you're willing to listen and willing to act, then you will change your life.

Problems don't go away, not on their own. No, you're going to have to look deep inside to see where you've been settling for less, then take action to step into your power. By that, I mean become the best version of you. It will be the greatest gift you ever give yourself. That's because when you take action, you clear away the pain, the doubt, the fear. You become the hero, the rock star of your life. When you rock, you can feel it. Everybody can. And it opens new doors with new opportunities—the opportunities you need to live your dream.

Look, I get it. You're doubting yourself. You have to be, or you wouldn't be reading this. That's okay. I used to put myself down and think I wasn't good enough. I used to believe I didn't deserve my dream, that it wasn't "realistic." It took me years and a lot of pain to figure out not only was my dream possible, but that I deserved to live it.

We have to give ourselves the tools we need to change—tools like a positive, can-do attitude, the resilience to overcome any obstacle, and the belief that it's never too late to change.

Who Am I?

I'm Alexander Woodrow, but everyone calls me "Woody." I'm a founding member of the rock band, Our Last Night. We formed in 2004 when we were in high school. Since then, we've built our band into a multi-million dollar business, which is a serious step up from living in a beat-up van, eating fast food every night, and being pressured by our parents to get "real jobs"... You know, the kind that pay the bills, but don't serve your dreams.

From our humble beginnings, our band's been able to generate millions of views, fans, and dollars—all without the help of a record label or a manager. We'd had them in the past, but they never worked out the way we expected them to. We thought we needed them, but in the end, we discovered we only needed each other and our fans. Since then, we've been able to grow our business and ourselves to the point where we can say we've reinvented how unsigned artists approach success in the music industry. But here's the thing: What we've done works for *any industry* and *any dream*, including yours. That's why I want to share what I've learned with you—none of it is music industry exclusive. Instead, it's exclusive to making YOU the best version of yourself, the version that will give you an incredible competitive edge no matter what dream you pursue.

Living a dream takes effort, that's why they're dreams and why they remain nothing more than that for so many... but that doesn't have to be true for you. Not if you're willing to put in the effort. Let this book be your foundation.

So how do you know you're ready to be a rock star?

You know you're ready if...

- You know there's more to life, but don't know where to look.
- You're doubting yourself or feel like you aren't good enough.
- You want to get clear about your dreams and not just achieve them, but live them.
- You're tired of feeling anxious, depressed, or stressed about what to do with your life.
- You want to feel good... all that mind-body-spirit stuff.

If you answered yes to any or all of these, then you're ready, the power is in your hands. Are you excited? I know I am, but first, let's get something straight: I wrote this book to empower you, but I'm not a guru. I don't even like that word. There's too many people manipulating others into thinking they know the "right" way to live.

I believe the power to change is already inside you. You gotta take the action to claim it yourself, and you gotta take it now, however that looks for you. Because we're all different. No one knows how you feel except you, just like no one knows what it's like to be you. You're going to fall on your ass a few times. Everyone does. That's life. The difference is how many times you're willing to pick yourself up to try again. Do it enough times, do it enough ways, and you'll get there. You'll live your dream.

Maybe you think that's easy for me to say, but I wasn't always a rock star. I was just a guy with a dream, and so was everybody else in my band. It took us over a decade to get our sound right and even longer to figure out how to market that sound to millions of people. If we can do it, you can do it.

I don't want you to make more mistakes than you have to. My intention is to share what I've found to be most helpful, not just in discovering a dream, but growing it while navigating through all the challenges life throws at us. I'm talking inevitable stuff like stress, anxiety, and wondering if we're ever going to make it. With what you're going to discover inside these pages and inside yourself, you're going to take your dream to the next level and start rocking your life how you want to—not just for today, not just for a few years, but forever. You deserve it. You deserve to have, to be, and to do everything you've ever wanted.

I'm going to show you how.

Gimme a "Hell yeah!" if you're ready to start living—I mean really living. Say it loud. Say it now. If you're in public and don't want to make a scene, you can say it in your head, but think it loud, really loud, like you're yelling in your head. *Feel it.* It's not enough just to say the words, you have to *feel* them.

All the love,
ALEXANDER "WOODY" WOODROW

YOU ARE THE
ROCK STAR

PART I

DREAM

Before we explore how to find and achieve your dream, ask yourself: How do you measure success? Because that's important. If you only measure success by money or material possessions, then it's going to be difficult for you to be happy because you'll never be fully satisfied; there will always be more money to make and more stuff to buy. It's not a healthy way to judge yourself because it doesn't represent anything about who you are, not where it counts—on the inside.

That's why I measure success by the ability to take charge of your life, to step up, to meet obstacles as opportunities, and to feel good about being your authentic, badass self. It's all about being comfortable with who you are and clear with what you want. And by "comfortable with who you are," I mean comfortable with the process of becoming the new rock star you, not with the old habits that are holding you back.

I know you might be thinking you have to make money

to be successful. Don't get me wrong, money is important. One of my favorite speakers, Zig Ziglar, said, *"Money isn't the most important thing in life, but it is reasonably close to air on the gotta have it scale."* Money is magnificent and you deserve to have tons! But if you're only after money or fame, I can't help you. However, if you're interested in meaning and purpose, in living your dream and feeling good about yourself, don't worry: Money will flow into your life.

Who you are is more important than what you have.

You can't take money or material stuff with you when you die, but you can take your rock star spirit, your knowledge that you lived your dream and made a difference in the lives of others.

Which brings me to my next point: Does your dream provide value to someone else? There's enough people trying to have expensive things and social status without giving anything in return. If you aren't trying to make the world better because you're in it, that's a recipe for mid-life crisis. Ask yourself: Without a life full of meaning, what's the point? And who creates that meaning?

YOU DO!

By following your dream, you get to create a life full of meaning. You get to be the person who makes this world a better place: for you, for me, for everyone. That's how to measure success. That's how you know your life rocks and the dream is real.

1

YOU ARE THE ROCK STAR

WE ALL HAVE an idea in our head of what a rock star is. Some might see an image of being on stage in front of thousands of people, some might see a person who gets all the girls or does a lot of drugs. We assume we know people and professions based on stereotypes. Sure, there are rock stars out there who fit the stereotypes in our mind, but not all of them are like that. So to make this book effective, we need to shift our definition of what a "rock star" is.

To me, a rock star is someone who goes after what they want, expressing themselves by whatever means they choose, striving to become the champion of their own existence. By that definition, being a rock star means stepping into your personal power. It means not living in fear of stress, doubt, or anxiety so you can get what's rightfully yours. It's about discovering what makes you come alive and going after it.

This book is designed to help you sort out the hard stuff so you can live the good stuff. Going after a dream takes work, but with the tools I'll be sharing, it should feel effortless. That's because it's all about going after what you want, being in alignment with your passion and purpose, in tune with that badass version of yourself that deserves to feel good being who you are.

Personally, I've had a difficult time embracing the idea of being a rock star. For a while, I compared myself to others and didn't think I was good enough. I'm in one of the biggest unsigned bands on the planet, but for the longest time, I beat myself up thinking I wasn't worthy, that I was a fraud, an imposter, and one day everyone would discover I wasn't a "real" musician. Have you ever felt like you weren't valuable, or worse, not allowed to follow your dream?

I did. For example, on Our Last Night's first studio album, the producer told me I wasn't good enough to record. That stunned me. I walked out of the studio thinking I was worthless, that if I didn't do the album, I must be a fraud. What if people found out? What would my friends and family say?

With the producer's words ringing in my ears, I fell into a state of depression. I actually questioned the point of my existence. It hurt, it hurt a lot—more than it needed to. Instead of rising to the challenge, I allowed myself to be defeated. I stayed in the band, but didn't feel like I was a part of it. It wasn't until I started owning my experience and using it as a lesson, one that inspired me to become the rock star of my own life. That was when I was able to stand out of my depressed state and learn to play better. I hadn't worked enough on my craft and the universe was guiding me to put in the effort to be the best version of me. I couldn't see it at the time. I couldn't see that it was meant to teach me more about life.

I needed to go through the process. A process that is necessary for us all. Learn from my mistakes and from yours. When you do, you'll discover the tremendous value you bring to the world, the value that brings you closer to living the dream you desire. This is the long way of saying that when I use the term, "rock star," I mean YOU, the rock star version of YOU. Whatever that is, whatever that looks like to you. You can do it!

A Note from the Author

A lot of self-help books end each chapter with a recap of the most important lessons in them. I want to do something different. I want you to ask questions based on what you've learned instead. When we ask ourselves questions, we get answers—answers that are deeply true and personal to us. Think about your answers, really think, and if you can, meditate on them. You may be surprised at what your subconscious reveals...

Questions to ask yourself:

- Can you think of a time you felt like you weren't good enough?
- Have you ever felt so deflated by the outcome of a situation that it makes you question the point of your existence?
- What stories are you telling yourself that aren't true?

2

FAILURE IS AN ILLUSION

WE'RE ALL GOING to fail. It's inevitable. When we try something new, we learn by failing. But many of us put ourselves down by thinking we aren't good enough—as if we're expected to master everything easily and if we don't, that we'll never be any good at it. But that's a lie. Quitting is the only point we ever truly fail. When we quit, we never allow ourselves to get better. Failure is an illusion; it's only purpose is to make us stronger by challenging us to try again. So whenever you tell yourself, "I can't," or "I'm not good enough," that's not true.

You're closer to your dream than you think. Get up, dust yourself off and get back into it. *We learn more from failure than from success.*

Everybody knows the story of how Thomas Edison invented the lightbulb, but not everyone realizes it took ten-thousand setbacks before he figured it out. The average "overnight success" doesn't come out of nowhere. It was true for Edison and it's true for us. What the media doesn't tell you is that most "overnight" celebrities spent years investing time and energy into learning their craft and mastering it—

appearing to fail and then getting back up to try again. They weren't lucky; they *created their own luck* by going after their goals over and over—regardless of setbacks or failures. There's power in persistence. Successful people learn from their mistakes. They get creative and keep right on going. That's how they get what they want; that's how their dream comes true.

Your circumstance doesn't define you, your reaction does.

It was May 14, 2015, and my band was in Stuttgart, Germany. We were a little over a month into our first world tour. It was a crazy, exciting time full of hope and enthusiasm. We were sharing a double-decker tour bus with a band called Palisades, and playing to packed venues every night. It was a dream come true...

Except for our driver, Simon. He was a heavy-set guy you could hear wheezing from across the room, and he would switch his mood in an instant when something pissed him off, which unfortunately was all the time. Even something as simple as us "talking too loud" or shutting the bus door "too hard." We were a young bunch of guys having the time of our lives; of course we were going to be loud! None of us liked him, but since he was only one small glitch in an otherwise perfect experience, we tolerated him... That proved to be a huge mistake.

As we walked off the bus to another sold-out venue, I'll always remember Simon leaning out the side door and waving cheerfully, shouting, "Have a great show!" I took a mental note how weird that was, and how Simon hadn't said anything nice in over a month. But instead of his sudden change in behavior setting off warning bells, I blew it off. Maybe the old grump was finally warming up to us...

I quickly put Simon out of my mind as we took the stage. The air was electric; the crowd went wild. Afterward, we were hanging out on the bus waiting to leave—only no Simon. We were so amped, we didn't think anything of it at first. We figured he was taking a nap.

Now usually, tour bus drivers sleep all day so they can drive all night. Simon's bed was behind a locked door that was part of the front cabin where he drove. The time was approaching three a.m. We called Simon's phone and texted, but got no answer. So we knocked on his door. We got nothing: no answer, no snoring, no sound at all. We began to expect the worst. Simon had been wheezing worse than usual lately. What if he'd had a heart attack and died in his sleep? We decided to break down the door. It didn't take much force, and to our surprise, Simon wasn't dead. He simply wasn't there.

Where could he be? Every driver knows to be on the bus and ready to roll out at call time, and it was way past that now. The guys and I were worried because every hour that passed meant we were less likely to find someone who could drive us to the next show—which was the biggest of the entire tour! We started brainstorming. Maybe Simon went for food and got mugged. If we found him in one piece, then maybe we could get going...

We decided to fan out and check the nearby restaurants, alleys, and bars. It began to rain, a real downpour. We checked the nearby pubs, we called the hospitals, and eventually we bit the bullet and called the police to file a missing person report. We were soaking wet and worried, uncertain what to do next.

Remember that band, Palisades, we were sharing the

tour bus with? That was when they came down from the second story of the bus and said, "Hey, this is gonna sound really weird, but all our money is gone! You better check yours too." We stared at them in disbelief. The money must have been misplaced. It couldn't be stolen.

Our tour manager opened the lock box where he kept our money. The yellow bag that held over $20,000 at the beginning of the night was empty. Everyone was stunned. Usually, our manager brings the box into the venue for safe-keeping, but this venue was so small, there was no backstage area to secure it... so he kept it on the bus. How did Simon know? Had he been planning to rob us all along?

We called the bus rental company. They refused to admit they were at fault or take responsibility for the missing funds. Then they added insult to injury by demanding we pay the remainder of our bus rental fee for the tour. Yeah, right! As if that was ever gonna happen. We immediately switched to a different rental company, and long story short, managed to finish the tour. To this day, we don't know where Simon went, or how far our $20k lasted him. There was no point suing him or the bus company. We'd have to do it in Germany, and none of us had the time or money to deal with that. Sometimes, you just have to let things go and be grateful for what you have. You can't let the past wreck your future.

Even when you think you've made it, there will be times you get knocked back down. What Simon did to us was a massive loss for us as individuals and as a business. The lesson was an expensive one, but we kept going. We didn't let Simon stop us. We didn't give in to our anger, our fear, our sadness. It wouldn't have helped. The only thing that helped was moving forward, and you know what? We made the next show, and the show after that, and we had a blast!

We finished the tour, not with the big payday we were expecting, but we still broke even. We got by and kept going.

The world will test you. It's part of making you the best version of yourself. As much as some of these lessons hurt, you need to keep moving. And if you feel pissed off, sad, or depressed, it's okay. It's normal. *Just keep moving.* That alone is a massive success, because that's where most people give up. Remember, your circumstances don't define you, your reactions do.

Questions to ask yourself:

- Are you letting your circumstances define you?
- In what ways have you learned from your setbacks?
- In what ways could you keep moving?

3

DEALING WITH HATERS AND TROLLS

HAVE YOU BEEN told your dream isn't realistic? That you should settle for less? Or that you're not good enough? Think about the people who told you these things. Put yourself in their shoes. How do they see the world? Now ask yourself:

- Are they happy?
- Are they living their dream?
- Do they even have a clue what they're talking about?

Most likely they don't, but even if they do, they don't know what it's like to be you. Try to understand them. If they love you, then they are speaking from a desire to protect you, to shield you from the unknown. Why? Because chances are they settled. They didn't get to live their dream, so they don't think you can either. Sometimes it's worse, and they want *their dream* to become yours. If you confuse someone else's dream for your own, you may not realize how bad a fit it is until it feels like it's too late to change. Of course, it never is, but it can feel that way. That's why you need to be sure the dream you're following is your own.

Then there are the haters, the online and real life trolls and bullies who want to bring you down. Unlike your loved ones, they aren't trying to protect you. They're trying to protect themselves by dragging you down to their level and making you just as miserable as them. They do this because most of the time, they've been treated poorly, and it's all they know. They're too afraid to chase their own dreams, so they focus on trying to destroy or shoot down the dreams of others. That's a sad way to live, but as any quick glance around will tell you, there are plenty of unhappy people in this world. It's not their fault, they just haven't discovered how to step out of their conditioning to create their dream.

If you try to do battle with the haters and trolls, it will be a waste of energy. After all, you might be able to convince the people who love you that your dream is worth pursuing, but the haters? No way! That doesn't mean we need to hate them back. So let them go, don't waste your time. If you can, love the haters. If you have them, it means you're doing something right—you're doing something that challenges their limited beliefs. Remember, your dream is for you, not them.

Questions to ask yourself:

- There are many ways we experience haters, can you think of a time when someone didn't understand you and projected their own insecurity onto you?
- Our dreams are our own, not everyone will

understand, have you been waiting for the support of others instead of supporting yourself?

- Getting reflections from others that challenge you is good, usually it means you are challenging them, notice if someone is trying to make you better or bring you down. Can you see it from their perspective?

4

TRIGGERING THE INTERNET

My band has pissed off a lot of people on the internet, whether it's our cover songs or our social media posts. There's that saying that any press is good press, and usually it is, as long as it's not career-ending. It's all good until it's not, and everyone seems to have thin skin these days—and I mean thin, like wet toilet paper! So be aware that what you post stays there and can be used against you later—years or even decades later. Try not to burn bridges, but at the same time, it's important to share your truth. Don't lay down for people to walk all over you.

I remember when our band covered a song people either loved or hated, and I mean *extremely hated*. So much so that we actually had people telling us they wish we died! Our lead singer, Trev, isn't one to "turn the other cheek," so he called them out via social media. Of course the internet was up in arms over his reply. But overall, Trev stood up and called someone out who deserved some karma coming his way. The joke was ultimately on the haters, because it made our cover go viral.

I think it's okay to trigger some folks. Nowadays, it's

impossible not to. Honestly, someone's probably triggered by me saying this! If that's you, let it go. It's a chance to grow. We're all reflections of each other, giving and getting the opportunity to learn more about ourselves and the world. Being triggered isn't about the other person, it's about the relationship you have with yourself and the relationship you have with what's being said. It's okay to ask yourself, "Why does this piss me off?"

If triggered, then before taking action, ask yourself how what you're posting or saying might positively or negatively affect others. Picking the wrong fight, or the right fight at the wrong time, can cost you opportunities. You may never realize how many until it's too late.

Karma is real. The more you help others, the more you celebrate their wins and support them through their struggles—the more people will notice and start to love you for it. As a result, you'll find yourself with more and more opportunities to level up your dream because you supported others.

One of the many epic laws of the universe states, "Give and you shall receive." If you want to receive, then *give*. Whether it's praise or respect, empathy or support, give it to others where it is due and you'll see it returned to you. Remember, as Winston Churchill said, "We make a living from what we get, but we make a life from what we give."

Think about that as you post and pursue your dream. How is what you're posting setting you up for success in the long term? We're all building a brand, and it's a balancing act of caring about the right things and letting the rest go. Stand up for yourself, share what you love rather than bashing what you hate. Do this while knowing that the virality of human nature is to promote things we love, but also things we hate. Choose your path, and choose it wisely.

Questions to ask yourself:

- If something triggers you know that its not the person saying it that is triggering you, its the relationship you have with what is being said. What can you learn?
- Do you primarily post about what you love, or bash what you hate?
- How have you experienced giving in your life? How does it feel?

5

FIGURING OUT WHAT YOU WANT

WE'VE TALKED ABOUT seeking your dream, but did you know your dream is also seeking you? The world put you here for a reason, so let's show it what you're capable of! You deserve to feel amazing, to be amazing, and to do amazing things.

The first thing to figure out is what's in your way. Most of the time for me, it's me—I'm in my own way. Meaning I'm either unclear, uncertain, or I don't believe in myself enough to go through the challenges of making it happen. What about you? When you look in the mirror, do you see your worst enemy or biggest fan? If you're not cheering yourself on, you're probably beating yourself up. Constructive criticism is fine, but what you don't want and don't need is the destructive kind. I'm talking about that voice in your head that tells you you can't, you're not good enough, and to give up because it's too hard. That kind of self-sabotage can hurt worse than any hater or troll because it comes from within.

We can pick up on these negative thought patterns from experiences, from our environment and the people we are with. We internalize them and let them become the rule of our reality. They're not true and therefore we create an illusion of what we can and cannot do.

We've all had this happen. Somewhere along the line we believed someone who was full of shit and we let it get to us. It's okay. It's part of life. Noticing we're doing it is the first step. Just be aware to start, you're greater than whatever is going on in your head and it doesn't serve you to talk crap about yourself.

Check your internal messaging. What are you telling yourself? What are you saying that you'd never dare let anyone else say to you? Whatever it is, observe it. Where is it coming from? Is it logical? Or is it a bunch of hateful nonsense? Stuff like, "I'll never live my dream," "I'm a loser," "Everybody hates me," is all crap. Once you observe yourself saying things that don't serve you, you can begin to rewire your thinking to encourage yourself instead of tear yourself down. I'll show you how.

Maybe your negative self-talk isn't as intense as we've made it seem but it's still holding you back. Perhaps it's convincing you that it's okay to keep putting off what you need to do until it's "the right time." Or possibly it's been going on for so long you've forgotten what your dream really is. Hey, we're human. It happens. Because dreams are so big, they're easy to put off or give up on. But just because you haven't acted on it yet, that doesn't mean your dream goes away. It's still there, waiting. Waiting for you to jump up and say, "I'm ready! Let's rock this!"

Achieving your dream is all about belief—the unwavering belief your dream will happen. You will live it. All it takes is belief to get the ball rolling. But believing isn't always easy. So to fix that, we're going to figure out everything you don't like about your life. This will help you get clear: First, on what your dream is, and second, to get you on the path to creating it. Some people spend their whole lives struggling with (or against) their dreams and never figure it out. Lucky for us we're about to.

Before I figured out what I wanted, I felt lost. I didn't know what I wanted, and I wasn't ready to listen to all the goal-setting advice my Dad was always trying to give me. It wasn't until I started looking at what I *didn't* want that I found out what I did.

Exercise: Finding My Dream

 Take out a blank sheet of paper and a pen. Draw a line down the middle of the page. Across the top write your name, then under it, write, "Finding My Dream." Now in the left-hand column, I want you to write the things you don't like about your life. Start with one specific area, like your job, school, or relationship.

You're going to be writing what you don't like about that part of your life. Getting it out of your head, onto the paper, then flipping it to create the opposite positive statement, like it's true for you already. This helps rewire the negative thought patterns that are holding you back.

Finding My Dream List

While making your list, feel free to include the things that make you angry, anxious, confused, stressed, scared, or pissed off. Just get it on the page and tell yourself what you don't want. At a minimum, create a list of at least five or six things you don't like (you can go longer if needed). Do your best to list all the most important things first. These are the things that come into your mind as recurring negative thought-loops. For example, if you choose your job, you might be saying, "Nobody appreciates me." If you choose your appearance, you might be thinking, "I'm ugly and I hate my body." If you choose your finances you might write, "I don't have enough money."

Once you have your dislike list done, look it over. Does seeing it on paper make you realize anything? Read your list again and realize you're way more badass than any negative ideas inside your head. If you're still not sure, that's okay because we're going to work on that in the next column. Now we're going to take your negatives and flip them into their positive opposites.

Let's go back to your list. For example, if you wrote, "Nobody appreciates me," flip it to, "I feel grateful people acknowledge me all the time." If you wrote, "I'm ugly and I hate my body," it would turn into something like, "I'm beautiful, I love and embrace my body because I am worthy of love." If you wrote, "I don't have enough money," shift it to "I am excited about the money I have and I always have enough to share and to spare." The idea is to create the opposite statement. Make it positive. Write it like you have achieved it already, and attach a healthy emotion to it. Emotions are a powerful way to shift our mindset from negative to positive. So have fun with this. What would you write if you could have, be, or do anything?

- **IMPORTANT:** Be sure to write the positive version in the present tense, as if you've already made the change, and attach a powerful, positive emotion to it. This will serve as the foundation for discovering your dream.

Everything you dislike belongs to the old you, and the

old you is transforming. The new you is being born, and that you is here to stay.

You are what you think. Your subconscious can't tell the difference between the truth and a lie. Whatever you tell it often enough, it believes. Chances are, like a lot of people, you've been beating yourself up thinking all kinds of negative things. That's because we judge ourselves more harshly than anyone else, and we're more reluctant to forgive ourselves. This negative self-talk is one of the key things that holds people back.

Don't worry. Your subconscious isn't stuck that way. We're going to fill it with who you want to be: your ideal self. *Your rock star self!* The subconscious will then work to make what we tell it real. It runs in the background like an app on your phone, helping generate enough confidence for you to take action and manifest your dream. How cool is that?

Remember, it's important that you write your positive affirmations in the present tense *as if they were already true*. None of this, "I wish I had," or "I want to be" wishy-washy crap. That kind of language takes power away from us and projects feelings of doubt. Doubt attracts more of the same, making it that much harder to get the rock star change you want into your life.

Put the power back in your hands with inspiring phrases like, "I am," "I have," or "I'm becoming...." Your subconscious is stubborn and looking for excuses not to change because change can be hard or even scary, but it's essential for growth. It's essential for upleveling your life.

Repeat this action down your entire list, transforming the negative to positive. Don't worry if you don't believe the positive list yet, just get it down on paper. When you're done, cross out all the things you dislike about your life. *Really cross them out.* Its okay to get mad. Cross them out because they no longer have a place in your life.

Get a new sheet of paper or turn the one you're using over, whichever is easier. Write your positive, present-tense statements on it. Feel free to decorate the paper, make it a reflection of you, epic, and fun to look at. Now put your list somewhere you'll see it every day, or make copies and stick them in multiple places. Good spots are:

- On the back of your bedroom door
- On your computer
- Next to your bed
- In the bathroom where you brush your teeth

The important thing is to see it every day. It doesn't matter if you actually read it, even though you might want to —after all, it's your future highlight reel! But putting it somewhere you see every day energizes both your conscious and subconscious mind. If you can, say the list out loud every day at least once, or say it in your head. The best times are right after you wake up and right before you go to bed, but anytime can work great.

Our brain is a magnet and what we focus on, we attract more of. So by putting your affirmations where you'll see them every day, you're training your subconscious to remember the goals you're working towards. This keeps us open to opportunities we might never have noticed before— opportunities to make the most out of life!

The best way to program your positive statements into your subconscious is to say them as *affirmations*. Say them with confidence, with strength, authority, and absolute belief. It works better if you say the words with conviction and energy. If you're having trouble believing the words, say your affirmations normally to start. Then, to the best of your ability, say them louder with authority. Can you feel the difference?

Speaking of feelings, if you feel anxious or scared during or after your affirmations, that's okay. Just breathe. The more powerful phrases always trigger emotional responses. Feel them, acknowledge them, and let them pass.

Questions to Ask Yourself:

- Which area of your life challenge you the most?
- What are the negative thoughts you tell yourself about your circumstance? (Use these to start your list.)
- How would it feel to live the way you want? (Use this as a guide when writing your positive present-tense statements.)

PART II

IMAGINE AND INVENT

DOES YOUR MIND ever feel scattered? Like you're lost at sea, floating with no direction, confused, and alone? That can be a hopeless reality if we don't give our mind something positive to focus on. Think of it as a boat without a captain, just floating along in a massive ocean, going any which way the tide goes. Pretend that's the normal setting of the mind, floating around with no purpose, no direction, no love for itself.

But put a captain on the ship, and now we're taking off! The captain creates *purpose* for the vessel. The boat goes where he focuses and maintains that course with love and care.

When we're crystal-clear about what we want, we give our mind a mission, a purpose, something positive to focus on and work towards. We create the direction by first knowing what we don't want, which we just figured out.

So what about you? You have your list. Look at it.

6

BEGINNER'S MINDSET

Figuring out who we are is a lifelong adventure. It's filled with clarity and confusion, ups and downs, constantly defining and redefining who we are. We all want to be good at what we do. No one wants to suck, but usually when we try something new, we aren't very good. Its okay. We start out as a beginner and we make mistakes, we make so many that we quickly learn what works and what doesn't. This process is one of the most important points in this book.

It's the process of being a beginner. It's beginner's mindset.

When you're a beginner, you're always learning. You're willing to try without the fear of not being good enough. Instead of quitting, you just say, "Well that didn't work, let's try this!" And you go on to the next step, expanding your consciousness in the process. Beginner's mindset allows you to create, to explore, and to stay open to the experience. You don't talk trash to yourself, you don't beat yourself up or allow doubt to set in.

You'll never know it all. Even when you master this skill or that, there's always something more to learn—or unlearn.

When you accept the idea that you'll never stop learning, that's when you'll create your best work. If you know everything, there's no room to grow. There's no space to learn more or be more. You'll be too busy trying to show off what you already know instead of being open to new opportunities. We see this a lot with people who practice something a certain way their entire life, then when someone presents a different, often better way, they aren't open to it. They write it off because they've filled their mental hard-drive up and there's no more space. There's no more room to grow.

Sometimes, your dream has to change and grow, just like you have to change and grow. Be ready to pivot when that happens. After all, not many people get to live their dream the way they first imagine it. That doesn't mean you don't get to live a different (and almost always better) version, but that only happens when you stay open to change. There are always ups and downs, whatever path we choose. The ups tend to follow the downs, making it important to keep going. There may come a time when an opportunity to pivot presents itself. That's not giving up. That's not selling out. It's staying open to opportunity, which is simply smart business.

For example, a few years ago, our old manager told us to do rock covers of pop songs on YouTube. We were super-against it, but he insisted it was the fastest, easiest way to get more eyeballs on our band. He said it was because people weren't searching for us, they were searching for their favorite songs by artists they already knew. "But we aren't a cover band!" was our defense, and it was a weak one, but it made sense to us at the time. We were coming at the idea from our own limited way of seeing the world.

Playing cover songs—being a "cover band"—was never the plan, never our dream. But once we decided to embrace a beginner's mindset and surrender to the experiment, we discovered the greatest promotional tool we've ever had. Cover songs took us from almost breaking up to becoming a multi-million dollar business, with the added bonus of getting our original songs in front of people who otherwise would never have heard them. And that, my friend, is why you need to be ready to pivot, to stay open to new ideas and new variations of your dream. Beginner's mindset can take you there.

Maintaining a beginner's mindset is a great tool to release stress. It frees you from the pressure of having to know everything all the time. It releases you from the need to prove anything. When you stay open to learning, you expand your ability to create what you desire.

Not too long ago, I walked into a Hollywood party feeling really intimidated. I didn't know anyone except the people who'd invited me. They were busy, so I tried small talk with the first person I met. Luckily, they were a musician too, so I started asking them questions about their music. I didn't say that I knew anything about music or that I played myself. Over the course of the conversation, I learned a lot about improvisational theory, which is a fancy term for playing music without knowing exactly what's going to happen. You create in the moment, like starting a conversation with a stranger.

If I had been more focused on sharing my knowledge instead of discovering his, I would have missed an opportunity to learn about a form of music I never knew I was interested in. Because I chose to embrace his ideas with a beginner's mindset, I not only learned a new musical theory but gained a new friend. How cool is that? There have been many times since where I took my beginner's mindset into a conversation and learned something new that expanded my view of the world.

Many experts talk about this idea of a beginner's mindset and how it's helped them. After spending years learning, they come back to the basics; they come back to being a beginner because that's where the creativity is, that's where massive expansion and growth is.

The beginner's mindset is something I can't emphasize enough. The beginner is the master and the master a beginner. Don't just accept things as they come; be curious. *Be inspired.* Keep your beginner's mindset close and stay open as you continue to turn your dream into reality.

Questions to ask yourself:

- Think about the areas of your life where you were a beginner: What was that like? Did you ask a lot of questions? Did you learn a lot?
- Where could you adopt a beginner's mindset and make something old feel new to you?
- Are you willing to suck at something to get better?

7

YOU NEED A BIGGER AMP

I'LL NEVER FORGET my Dad holding back tears as he apologized for not believing in my dream. I'd worked all summer to save up for my first real big amp, the kind that could be heard over a drum kit rather than drowned out by one. I needed it for the local gigs my band was about to play, especially if we were to stand a chance of winning the battle of the bands.

I spent everything I had on my new amp. I was proud. It was exactly what I needed to step up my game, to get me one step closer to my dream. But when I got home, my Dad did not share in my excitement. He was frustrated and confused. He couldn't understand why I'd spent all my money on an amp when I was getting ready to leave for college.

As any dad would be, he was looking out for my best interests. Every parent wants their child to be successful, even if they won't admit it. When we do something that tests their ability to understand our actions, they feel challenged and frustrated. This makes them want to impose their often limited and conditioned belief systems on us, which to be fair, is what most of us do when we're challenged.

I like to think we're our parent's best teachers, or best challengers. Right or wrong, we naturally want to do the opposite of what they say because that's how we learn. How do you know what's right or wrong? The key is to stay true to you. I know you're probably thinking, "How the heck do I do that?"

Think of it like this: I worked hard to save up for my first big amp. It felt good when I got it. I knew what I wanted and I made it happen. Sure, my Dad's disapproval hurt and created self-doubt within myself. If I'd listened to him and returned the amp, that would have been the safe thing to do, and to many people, the smart thing. Everything between us would have been smoothed over in the short term, but the regret I would have felt over caving in to his concern... That's something I would have carried with me for years. My entire life might have been different. I might be a doctor or lawyer now, or have some other job that wasn't true to me. I wouldn't be the rock star I am today.

But I didn't listen. I kept that amp, and hung on to my dream.

A few weeks later, after we won the battle of the bands, my Dad came up to me and said, "Son, you need a bigger amp!" I laughed and hugged him, relieved there was no more confusion for him or for me. My dad got it now. He became a believer, and there's no better feeling than that.

Our parents want us to succeed, only they don't always know the best ways to support us. They may think they do, but they're still trying to figure life out, just like us. Staying true to yourself and your vision is what helps in the face of criticism and disappointment.

Doubt and negativity are always toughest when they come from the people closest to us. Learning to navigate through it and respond graciously is one of the hardest things you'll do. Nothing speaks louder to your critics than success, but be aware that for some, your success may harden them against you even more. The thing to understand is their jealousy says everything about them and nothing about you. These people resent your success because they refuse to pursue their own.

That's why it's one of the worst mistakes you can make to rely solely on friends and family for validation and support. If you get it, great, but that's not the case for many. A lot of friends and family won't understand. They may even try to hold you back and discourage you. Most don't mean to hurt you, but if you're counting on them to believe and they let you down, it's going to hurt. Release that expectation. You need to stand true in your belief, honor your vision, and do what YOU feel is right.

Find people that believe with you. In my band, we all believed in our success before there was anything to see. There are people who want you to succeed. Search for them and know they're searching for you. If you don't have them yet, it's okay. You'll find them, so keep the faith.

Questions to ask yourself:

- Are you waiting on the support of others to go after your dream? If so, what steps can you take to support yourself and create positive momentum towards what you're creating?
- Do you let other people's doubt and insecurity

govern your faith in yourself? Do you let others dictate who you are becoming?

- What is one thing you believed in and made come true even when others didn't think you'd succeed?

8

COMPARING YOURSELF TO OTHERS

THERE ARE a lot of things that can derail your dream, but the most toxic is comparing yourself to others. That's a good way to end up angry, jealous, or depressed. So why do it? Because it's how we're wired. We're predisposed to do it in our society. It's what we're thrown into as human beings... and we must overcome it.

Comparison is an easy trap to fall into—maybe the easiest. When you're first starting out, you can't compare where you are now to where the biggest people or players in your industry are. Take me for example. I'm a bass player. There's a lot of famous bass players I could have compared myself to when I was younger:

- Paul McCartney from The Beatles
- John Paul Jones from Led Zeppelin
- Gene Simmons from KISS
- Sting from The Police
- Flea from The Red Hot Chili Peppers

And the list goes on... These guys are legends and

among the greatest bass players in rock and roll history. Comparing myself to them when I was in my first battle of the bands, or even now, would be a big mistake. They are where they are, and I am where I am.

I've got a lot to be proud of, but it wouldn't feel that way if I sat around wondering why I wasn't as rich and famous as my heroes. In fact, it would make me feel miserable! Which is ridiculous considering all I have to be grateful for. So who do I compare myself to instead?

Myself.

The only person you should be comparing yourself to (or competing against) is yourself. I say that for one simple reason: It's the only healthy comparison and competition there is. If you're always trying to outdo yourself, you'll get better, and you'll be excited to do it. Why? Because you know you can! But if you try to compare or compete against your heroes or rivals, that never works. What they do and how far they go is out of your control. That's why it fails. You can only control what you can control, and that's you.

The truth is, some people are going to be further ahead than you, especially if they've been chasing their dream longer. Watch what they do, take notes. Use them as inspiration but not comparison. There will only ever be one of you just like there will only be one of them. Your triumph lies in your ability to realize you are unique, your voice is unique, and your presence is one of a kind. Everyone is on their own path with different resources, skill levels and connections. Successful people know it's less about skill or talent and more about how creative you are with what you have and owning it.

There is more than one way to get what we want; we just have to find what works best for us. If you make small progress each day, it adds up over time. Pretty soon, all those small victories will turn into a major triumph. By believing that—by knowing it—you'll embrace the process more and compare yourself less. Let me put it another way: You step into your true self when you realize who you are is enough. And you become aware that the road to success is paved by learning from others and being uniquely you. So if you're feeling overwhelmed or like you're not good enough, remember, the only person to compare yourself to is yourself. Strive for consistent, small steps. You don't tour the world in a day. You do it by playing one show at a time, one song at a time, one part at a time. If you can do that, you'll get there. You'll live your dream.

Questions to ask yourself:

- In what ways do you compare yourself to others?
- Could you do a better job of trying to outdo yourself rather than outdo others?
- Success is less about skill and talent and more about what you do with what you have, knowing this, what could you do with what you have now that would get you closer to living the positive statements you listed in the Finding My Dream exercise?

PART III

BELIEVE AND ACHIEVE

THE MIND is what separates us from all other animals on the planet. What we believe we achieve, and in a full circle kind of way, what we achieve has a lot to do with what we think we're capable of. *This is the power of faith.* The belief that when we set our mind to something, we can and will make it happen.

We don't always have the ability to see the big picture, to know the how, the why, or the when. But we always have the ability to create more of what we focus on. We always have the ability to use our mind as a tool—a tool to help us become the rock stars we were born to be.

9

THE SHIFT

Do YOU EVER find yourself wondering, "Why me?" It happens. The world can throw some crazy stuff at us and it's easy to fall into victim mode. I like to think that we only get what we have the ability to handle...even if it feels overwhelming. Life happens for us, not to us. If something is roughing you up, I'm willing to bet it's really there to help you grow. So if you still find yourself thinking, "Why me?" I want you to say, "Try Me!" instead. This will give you the edge to meet life's challenges like a rock star.

Notice the difference in feeling when you say "Try Me," instead of "Why Me." This shift in mindset guides us to take action. Remember, the world doesn't happen TO you it happens FOR you. It's true. All that dumb, horrible, and annoying stuff is actually here to make us better. To help us be greater, rock harder, and stay open to new ways of experiencing the world.

You are not your circumstance. You are much greater—more than you know. But where most of us stumble is thinking that what happened to us defines us. So we let unfortunate, unwanted experiences dictate what we do, who we believe we are, and where we are going. By doing this, we create a more difficult reality by dwelling on the past. This is one way we depress our energy. If we fall into a "victim mentality," it becomes easy to live in a negative mindset. It becomes easy to dwell on the bad stuff because it takes less energy to stay stuck in the past. It takes action and energy to change. That's why going from "Why me?" to "Try me!" is so powerful. It creates a massive mental shift that puts you in an action-based mindset. That mindset can quickly liberate you from the chains of the past.

When we shift our mindset from victim to victor, the world becomes a little brighter. Seeing the world in a negative way is only expecting more negative stuff to happen. We all have people in our lives who dwell on the negative. Some of the phrases they like to use are, "I'm unlucky," or "I never win." This attracts more of the same. We get what we're looking for; we get what we're expecting. Living in a victim mentality attracts more of the stuff we don't want into our life because we're choosing to frame our experience as negative. The world is what you make it. If you look at everything through the lens of negativity, it looks negative!

When our perception is coming from a negative space, it will always guide us to see the worst in everything we do. So while I was depressed thinking about not recording that album, I began to think I didn't bring value to my band, then about how I didn't matter to the world, and finally, how I was worthless even to myself. Talk about down the rabbit hole! But it happens. I wish someone had told me back then that this experience wasn't about any of that. It was about challenging me to be better, to be more dedicated to my craft. The world will push us, and it's up to us whether we fall into victim mode or if we choose to see an obstacle as an opportunity to become better.

So remember, it isn't "Why me?" it's "TRY ME!" Most of the limits we create are made in our mind. They are there to help us grow, to be reframed, so we can be more effective at going after what we want in our own unique way.

So do it now. Make the shift.

Step into your power.

Questions to ask yourself:

- Can you think of a negative experience that made you step up your game and become better? What was that like? How did that make you feel?
- Do you have a "why me?" frame of my mind about something in your life right now? Meet it with a "try me" mentality and step up! Take note of each time you make a conscious decision to make this shift.
- What are some positive things you can tell yourself that would better align your beliefs with your "Finding My Dream" list?

10

YOU'RE RIGHT WHERE YOU'RE SUPPOSED TO BE

WE'RE ALL A PRODUCT of the influences we've had in our life. Who we choose to be surrounded by plays a massive role in who we become. When we imitate our role models, we fantasize about being them. We step into their energy and get a small taste of what their life is like. This helps us grow into our dream. In a way, we're tapping into their charisma, their genius, their unique style, and allowing it to inspire our own.

For example, I used to watch the bass players of my favorite bands growing up. Not necessarily their musicianship, but their charisma. I was fascinated by their stage presence: How they looked, how they acted, how they held themselves. I took it all in, allowing it to shape me as a performer. I became who I am today by observing and adapting those parts of my favorite bass players' charisma, blending and shaping them into what became who I am on stage and how I perform.

Maybe you're wondering how you know when you're trying to be someone you're not? There's a difference between stealing from someone and being inspired. There's an old expression from comedian Stephen Wright that goes like this: "To steal ideas from one person is plagiarism; to steal from many is research." There's no such thing as being completely original. Everything comes from the combination of everything we've ever been influenced or inspired by.

For me, one of those inspirations was Tupac. As a teen, I had all of his albums and even wrote a fifteen-page research essay on him in English class! One of his quotes stays with me and has proven to be a guide on my journey:

"I'm not saying I'm gonna change the world, but I guarantee you that I will spark the brain that will change the world. And that's our job, It's to spark somebody else watching us."

It's a powerful message, and so very true. What you do today could inspire the next generation tomorrow.

We get inspired by watching others, talking to others, and being around them. We take parts from them to add to our uniqueness, not replace it. Social media is a great example of this. We observe what someone else is doing and if we like the content, we mimic it to see if it works for us. Often times, it does seem like stealing, but there can be no other us, so our content is going to be unique to who we are as long we stay true to our ourselves and true to our purpose —the same purpose we discovered while making your dream list.

Stealing happens when we copy what someone else has without putting our own spin on it. This is detrimental to our growth because we're not being inspired. Instead, we're aligning ourselves with the feeling of not being good enough, that our life isn't as good as theirs, so we need to *be* them. We're not here to be copycats.

For example, to create *Star Wars*, George Lucas combined elements of *Flash Gordon*, a Japanese samurai movie called *The Hidden Fortress*, and most importantly, the theories about what makes mythology work from his college professor, Joseph Campbell. You see what he did? He took bits and pieces from different sources, combined them in new and interesting ways, then merged them with his own ideas. The result? An instant, multi-billion dollar franchise that's lasted decades and, let's face it, will likely last forever. Does that make George a copycat or a genius? I think you know the answer.

So if you're wondering, "Am I trying to be someone I'm not?" Ask yourself, "Is this an expression of my authentic self?" If yes, then it's all good. You're expressing yourself from your unique perspective. If no, or you're not sure, take a look at the people you look up to. What character traits do they embody? What can you learn from them?

You don't need to be anyone else, you need to be you. And the world needs you, in your highest expression of yourself. So take notes, apply what you like, and be the best version of you. No one else can.

While we're learning from others to discover who we are, it is possible to feel like an imposter. We all feel it at some point in our lives and it's totally normal when we first set out to chase our dream. That's because we're learning, we don't know exactly what's going to happen or when. So we just do what other people are doing. We have to go through the process. In the beginning, you won't have the answers. You might not know what's cool, or how everything works, or who you want to be, but believe it or not, that puts you at an advantage. You're not an imposter, you're just someone learning what works and what doesn't. Remember that beginner's mindset. Understanding that will help you grow. You're not a failure if things don't immediately go the way you thought they should. A dream isn't a sprint, it's a marathon. There's no need to rush. Embrace the moments as they come and be okay with watching and learning from others.

You're right where you're supposed to be, and with a little more action, you'll get to the next level, and the next and the next. Always growing, always learning and getting better.

Questions to ask yourself:

- How have you been influenced in your life by others? Have you been trying to be someone else, or have you been trying to learn from them how to better express yourself?
- Who inspires you? What is it about them that makes you want to be like them?
- Do you ever feel like you aren't where you're supposed to be? Take a mental note each time this happens. What steps can you take to make progress and keep going?

11

FAKE IT TILL YOU MAKE IT

HAVE YOU HEARD THE PHRASE, "Fake it till you make it?" Even if you don't feel like a success now, nobody knows that unless you tell them. Pretend you're successful. People react positively when you project confidence. They're more likely to listen and believe in you.

Note I said confidence, not arrogance. Arrogance might make you feel better now, but being an arrogant ass pretending to be something you're not is just asking for a lesson in humility. When you're building a sustainable long-term dream, arrogance doesn't project what you're working to create. It's about how you meet life's challenges and manage your personal growth. To put it another way, you're transforming your dream into reality by transforming yourself into your dream. Does that make sense?

Our dream can only grow as much as we grow. This is important. We must always be learning to live a life of purpose and meaning. That means we have to stay open, even if what we're about to do scares us.

I learned this at a young age. One of the first childhood memories I have is sitting at my first grade desk. It was a bright sunny day, the room seemed huge, and there were tons of colors everywhere. The excitement of being in school hadn't worn off yet, and I remember swinging my feet back and forth at my desk because my legs were too small to touch the floor. I was eager to raise my hand and answer any questions the teacher asked, regardless of whether or not I knew the answer.

That day we were discussing talents and the topic of tap dancing came up. I'll never forget my teacher asking, "Can anyone in our class tap dance?" My hand shot up. I didn't think I would actually be called on, I just had to get my hand up there. When she did call on me, I felt a rush. I got picked! It was exhilarating. Then, once the excitement wore off, the real "oh shit" moment kicked in. My teacher asked me to come to the front of the room and demonstrate.

My stomach sank. I felt heavy. I began to sweat and could feel my heart beating way too loud. But I couldn't back out. I was in too deep, so I walked to the front of the room, dreading every step.

I turned to face the class, desperate to hide my guilt. The teacher gave me a look of encouragement. I couldn't disappoint her. More than that, I couldn't disappoint myself. I decided to own it. I decided to tap dance the way I'd seen people do it in movies. How hard could it be?

I went all in with my best imitation. I must have looked ridiculous, but in that moment, I *believed* I knew what I was doing. And no one dared question my little blonde-haired, overall-wearing self. A kid with confidence is a powerful thing.

When I stopped, I looked at my teacher and to my delight she said, "Very good, Woody!"

I walked back to my seat with my head held high.

Fake it till you make it. It works!

Let me tell you about another time I decided to fake it, this time in front of my entire high school. It was one of my band's first gigs and it was in our high school auditorium. As I stepped on stage, I had no idea what was about to happen, only that I felt the need to do something epic. I saw a small amp and decided to do a backflip off it with my bass guitar. No practice, no nothing, just spur of the moment. My intuition kicked in, warning, "You can't even do a normal backflip! What makes you think you can do one with your bass?"

But I didn't listen. I let my adrenaline take control, stepping onto the amp. I told myself. "I'm doing this."

The song built, I closed my eyes, jumped, and tucked.

As I landed on my head, it was like the entire stage had just punched me in the face. I stood up in a daze. I couldn't feel my left leg, my shoulder was on fire, and a piece of my guitar was rolling across the stage. I couldn't hear much of what was going on. Everything was in slow motion, with a high pitched ringing in my ears... Somehow, I played it cool and finished the song.

Falling on my face in front of 300 people was not the result I'd hoped for. Surprisingly, after the show, people were impressed. I was a little confused, so I asked them what they meant. Apparently, I had done the flip with so much confidence, people assumed I did it all the time. Like it was no big deal. When I got back up and played it off, I guess that must have been what convinced them it was part of my act. I messed up, but kept going and they bought it. Whether on stage or in life, sometimes we mess up. How we own our mistakes and continue moving towards our goal speaks louder than any mistake. If you're confident and keep moving, most people won't even know anything went wrong.

Be willing to try. Be willing to fail. Be willing to own it.

Questions to ask yourself:

- How are you transforming your dream into reality? Are you trying to force the world to change or are you allowing yourself to become the type of person that fits your dream?
- Can you think of a time you had no idea what you were doing but did it anyway? How did that turn out?
- How could you practice being more confident in your everyday life?

12

WHAT I WISH I KNEW IN HIGH SCHOOL

ALL TOO OFTEN WHEN we pursue a dream, we focus on the end result. Most people fumble around, not really sure what to do. They get discouraged when they don't see instant results, then get so frustrated by their lack of progress that they give up on their dream altogether. But it doesn't have to be like that, not if you know the secret to setting goals.

If you've made it this far, hopefully, you're more clear about what your dream is and what you want out of life. Now it's time to revisit your *Finding My Dream List*. Are the goals you set vague or were they specific? An example of vague might be, "I feel good about myself." or "I am happy" or "I get paid to do what I love." These are great long-term lifestyle goals, but how quickly we create them depends on how specific we are.

For instance, what makes you happy and why? How much do you want to get paid? Where do you want to live and in what kind of house? Ask your goals specific questions that demand specific answers. This is your life design. Be specific and be clear. The more detail you provide, the more clear your path becomes, and the quicker you'll create it.

Providing a ton of detail might seem annoying at first, but it's one of the most powerful strategies to goal setting. Clearly defined goals identify what steps you need to take to move towards your goal. Breaking each step into smaller, bite-size goals is the key to success.

Don't stress if you can't see your goals right away or in the level of detail you'd like. We don't always know exactly *how* we're going to do something, we just need to decide *where* we're going, then commit to it. Often, the "how" reveals itself simply by taking positive action. That's because the world moves for the person on the go. So make a decision. Commit to taking some small, positive action today, then keep going. See where it takes you. Keep going with an open heart and an open mind; be ready to embrace the opportunities that present themselves.

The path to our dreams is paved with small, attainable goals. Taking them one by one is how we get the big stuff, the rock star stuff. Small goals are the words we learn before writing a sentence, the notes we learn before creating a song, and the experiences that lead us to our dream. These create the journey to the lifestyle shift we desire.

How do smaller goals work? They're like the headlights of a car at night; they break the trip down into smaller increments so you only focus on what's in front of you. You might have an address in the GPS, but if you've never been there before, you're trusting the computer will lead you there. You take one direction then another, knowing you're clear with where you're going. You have to execute twists and turns. You have to be aware of traffic, weather, and other hazards. For some, the road is quick, for others, it can seem like it goes on forever.

There are an incredible number of ways to get to the same place. So continue to trust, even when you make a wrong turn. The GPS adjusts itself, and you keep going with the belief you'll get to your destination. Think about that... You trust an app, a cell phone, and a satellite without even thinking about it. Imagine if that faith were placed in your dreams. Your goals. Turn after turn. Trusting the road will keep going, letting your faith guide you like headlights in the night.

If you did the *Finding My Dream* exercise in chapter five, then you've already taken action. If you didn't do the exercise, maybe now you understand how important it is. Go back and do it. You need to know what you want in order to get it. You need to know the direction you are traveling in.

If you've done the exercise but are still feeling uncertain, go back and try again. This isn't a one time thing, it's a process. Go back, think about what you don't like about one specific area of your life, and write it down. Then flip it like we did earlier—make it present-tense and positive with a healthy emotion attached to it. You can do this for any and all areas of your life, but start with one.

If you already know your dream, awesome! Keep taking action.

Go back and breakdown your positive affirmations into action-oriented chunks. Be specific. Ask yourself how you can make small steps toward your goals. Remember, large goals are achieved by completing smaller ones.

For example, if you wrote, "Nobody appreciates me," and flipped it to, "I feel grateful people acknowledge me all the time," you can then make a smaller goal that says, "I tell myself I'm appreciated when I wake up everyday."

If you wrote, "I'm ugly and I hate my body," and flipped it to, "I'm beautiful and love my body," you could break that down to, "I tell myself I am beautiful three times a day and I exercise my body in healthy ways at least three times a week."

If you wrote, "I don't have enough money," and shifted it to "I am excited about the money I have and always have enough money to share and to spare," you could write, "I made an extra $500 this month," and write yourself a check with a date on it for when you will receive that money.

Don't believe it works? Jim Carrey was once a broke and out-of-work Hollywood actor, but he believed he was going to be a movie star. He wrote himself a check for ten million dollars and dated it out what he considered to be a reasonable time frame. During that time, he hustled to get work; he didn't wait for a miracle. He knew if he worked for it, his dream would meet him halfway. And you know what? Right before the date on the check passed, he got that ten million dollar movie role, and the rest is history!

Get specific. The more clear you are with your dream, the better. Its okay to revisit your list. The list gives clarity, the list helps discover deeper meaning and purpose, and will guide you. Remember, the more specific and clear you are, the faster and easier you will create your dream.

Questions to ask yourself:

- Are you setting your goals in attainable ways, with bite-sized parts you can manage?
- Are you taking daily action to achieve your goals?
- Are you being as clear and specific as you can with your goals?

13

LOSING MY CONCERT VIRGINITY

ONE OF THE MOST important concepts in this book is the world happens *for* us, not *to* us. This simple shift in our thinking provides a quantum leap toward success. Trusting that epic things can and will happen for us (and that we deserve them) keeps us open to the amazing people, places, and situations that can change our lives forever.

Let me give you an example. I was in high school, and my friends and I were on our way from New Hampshire to Boston. I was so excited, I could barely sit still. We were going to see our favorite band, Sum 41, play live. They had made it big after releasing the album, *All Killer, No Filler*, and were staging an exclusive event near Fenway Park. It was sold out, but that didn't stop us. No way! My friends and I figured if we hung around outside, maybe we could meet the band after the show...

When we got to the event, we saw Sum 41's tour bus. It was straight out of the movies, a shrine on wheels, housing the legends we listened to every day. Like a moth drawn to a flame, we moved toward the bus. At that moment, the goal was to get close to the bus, to touch it and be close to greatness.

Then, as if someone was waiting for us to get there, the bus door opened. A tall man stepped out. We didn't recognize him, but the laminated tour badge around his neck told us he was important. The man took two steps toward us, looked right at me, and asked, "You guys want in? Give me your names."

My buddies and I stared at each other in disbelief. Was this guy serious? We quickly shouted our names and he told us to go to the show's entrance. In a few minutes, we could get in. Just like that, we were on the guest list.

I'll never forget seeing Sum 41 on stage. They were larger than life. Their presence was intoxicating, you couldn't look away, and the music! We knew every word. The band was so confident and real, I felt like I knew them. From that moment on, I knew what my dream was: I wanted to be on stage. I wanted to connect with people.

To be a rock star.

My band, Our Last Night, wasn't formed until two years later, but that was the night—the magic night my dream was born. I'm just a normal kid from a small town in New Hampshire, about as far away from the fame and fortune of the music industry as possible. Not many musicians from my state make it. But that didn't stop me, and it didn't stop the rest of the guys in my band.

When the biggest booking agent in our genre told us we were worthless, we didn't quit. When a show promoter said we weren't even worth $1, we didn't let it stop us. If we'd listened to everyone who hated us, where would we be? We would've been left wondering...

- What if we'd kept going?
- What if we made millions of fans?
- What if we had continued to chase our dream?

Everyone has to start somewhere, just like every dream has to start somewhere. Don't let where you are now stop you from getting where you need to be. Believe in something bigger.

If I can do it, why not you? Someone has to discover their dream and live it. There's always room for another rock star, and I don't just mean up on the stage, I mean in every field. Why can't it be you? What do the power players in your profession have that you don't?

I know you might be thinking they have talent, good looks, or wealthy connections, but even if they do, the truth is, they made a decision. They went for it and committed themselves to their dream.

So can you.

We're all trying to figure it out. There's always more to do, more room to grow, because that's why we're here. To become the biggest, most badass versions of ourselves. I believe in you. You can create the life you want. People do it every day. People just like you, everywhere and from all walks of life.

Now it's your turn.

Questions to ask yourself:

- Think of a time you were inspired. What did that feel like? What were you doing?
- How have your experiences helped create who you are?

- Think of a time you were criticized, can you use that as motivation?

14

TAKE ACTION

I FIRST LEARNED of Lisa Nichols in the movie *The Secret,* where she talked about the Law of Attraction and how to get what you want. Funny enough, my Mom felt so strongly about the movie that she actually paid me to watch it. I guess it was her way of getting me to pay attention. And she was right. From the very beginning, I was hooked, intoxicated by this idea, this power, called the Law Of Attraction. The Law states that like attracts like, so whatever we think becomes our reality—whether positive or negative.

Almost a decade later, I saw Lisa speak at a conference and that's when I realized her unique ability to impact others in deep and meaningful ways. I remember thinking, "Wow, this woman is a true rock star!"

One of the most powerful points Lisa made that day was that *investing in yourself isn't selfish.* It's actually selfish not to invest in yourself. That's because it's a disservice to those around you not to give them the best version of you. We want the people we learn from to always be learning, right? I know I do. I don't want to learn from someone who is stagnant or thinks they know everything. I want to learn from someone who's an expert at being a beginner, a constant student of people and of life.

Most people think of money when they hear the word investment, but that's not the only kind. There are all kinds of investments you can make in yourself: education, energy, faith, time, and they each reward you in their own way. Never let money be the thing that holds you back.

For example, I made an investment in myself for private coaching in Lisa's speaker's mastermind. In it, she was offering to teach me tons about speaking, business, writing, and self-development. All things I was excited to learn to help me in the music business and beyond. But it was a lot of money. I remember worrying if it was a smart decision, as it was one of the largest investments I'd ever made in myself. Would it be worth it? Would I get equal value? I also wondered, what if I didn't do it? Who would be missing out more? Me, or the people I could serve?

When we make investments in ourselves, a lot of emotion comes up. Usually, it's old conditioning with money, self-doubt, or worrying if we're making the right decision. I sat with the feeling of having made the investment already. As I thought about it, I noticed a feeling of excitement coming over my body. When I switched to thinking about not doing it, a feeling of depression crept over me, like I'd missed out on something important. That was enough for me. Clearly, my gut was telling me it was time. Time to make the investment.

As a part of my training, I attended one of Lisa's conferences in San Diego. She likes to create an experience, so her events are always epic, with tons of dancing, inspiring content, and legendary self-development exercises.

Upon entering the conference, I found a seat toward the back of the room. While Lisa was speaking, she looked through the crowd. When her eyes locked onto mine, I felt a rush. She paused mid-sentence and said, "Oh hey, honey!" with a wave. It felt great she remembered me.

At the next break, one of her assistants came up to me and said, "Lisa wants you to speak on stage in ten minutes. You ready?"

Before I had time to process the question, I said yes. It was like first grade all over again, only this time I wouldn't be tap dancing in front of a bunch of kids, I'd be speaking to thousands of people, both in the room and streaming live. I was terrified. What was I thinking? What had I gotten myself into? I was too blindsided to do anything but nod. I followed the assistant backstage. Self-doubt haunted me with every step. What would I say? How should I start? What if I lost my train of thought while I was on stage?

Before I could open my mouth to say maybe this wasn't a good idea, her assistant was gone. I was left backstage with nothing but my fear. It was at this point I realized it was too late to back out. I only had a few minutes to prepare, and if I didn't want to embarass myself and Lisa, I needed to clear my mind along with my nerves.

I took slow, deep breaths, remembering the first yoga class I ever led. Focusing on my breath had helped me overcome my fear then, and it would help me now. Breathe in, breathe out... In through the nose, out through the mouth. A smile crept over my face. Just like first grade, I knew what I had to do.

Take action.

As I walked on stage, I thought about the thousands of people I'd been in front of as a musician. I was used to that kind of crowd, but this—this was way different. This wasn't me playing with my band, having weeks to prepare, knowing the material inside and out. This was me in front of thousands of people with no idea what to do or what to say.

I decided to go with what I knew could never be wrong: my own experience. I shared some of the trials and tribulations my band faced over the past fifteen years. I told everyone how we'd been robbed of thousands of dollars, signed to a record label who didn't care about us, and how we had to overcome self-doubt by letting our music and our character speak for itself.

I spoke of how for the longest time I didn't believe in myself because I would constantly compare myself to others. Being in a band with phenomenal musicians had made me think I wasn't as good as they were and I let that thinking dictate my confidence, my creativity, and how I expressed myself.

My speech wasn't perfect, but the crowd loved it. For the rest of the event, I had people coming up to me saying how much they appreciated what I said. They didn't know how terrified and uncertain I'd been, or how close I'd come to saying no to the opportunity.

When we say yes to opportunities we say yes to growing. I'm not going to tell you to "just believe in yourself." That's cliche. I'm saying take action. That's what I wish I knew when I first learned about the Law of Attraction. We can sit and wish for everything, but if we aren't willing to take action to make it happen, it won't happen. So take action; action is where the magic happens.

Doors open when we say yes.

Doors open, and all we have to do is walk through them.

Questions to ask yourself:

- What kinds of investments are you making in yourself? They don't always have to be money, sometimes it's just taking the time to go for a walk and clear your head.
- Think of a time you did something that scared you; how did you feel after?
- How can you take action to live the dream you're creating?

15

YOUR INNER CRITIC

When I sat down to write this book, it felt as if everyone who'd ever doubted me was climbing on my back screaming, "You're not good enough! What have you ever done to write a book about achieving your dreams, let alone anyone else's? You're a fraud, Woody! A fake!" Fortunately, I was far enough along in my journey to understand doubt and fear are a normal part of growing up. But that wasn't always the case.

Growing up, I had a different dream than being in a band. I wanted to play major league baseball. I lived for the game, and was good enough to make starting catcher on my high school's varsity team. I loved it, but I was juggling two dreams by then... baseball and music. That's where the trouble started.

My band had been invited to perform at a show in Burlington, Vermont, which was four hours away. If we took the gig, we'd be opening for a much bigger band. This was a huge opportunity for us. It would be our first ever real show. We had played local gigs, but nothing that would compare to opening for Senses Fail, a nationally touring act and a band we all listened to and loved. Plus, it was a sold-out show. We'd be playing in front of 800 people. We had to do it. This was what I had dreamed of ever since I saw Sum 41 play as a younger kid. The only catch, my varsity team had our first home game the same day. The show was so far away, there was no way I could do both, so I had to choose, my team or my band.

We were favorites to make it to the state championship that year, and I hated to let my team down... but I couldn't disappoint my band either. I was torn. It felt like I had to trade one dream for another, and that hurt. My inner critic hit me left and right, first telling me my coach would bench me if I missed the big game, that I'd never make the major leagues, then it told me, "You'll never make it as a band, you suck, and if you get up on that stage, everyone will know it!"

But the whole time my inner critic was talking, I knew what I had to do. I had to follow my heart, and my heart was in music now. I mustered up the courage to pull my coach aside. I said, "I'm sorry, Coach but something came up. I've got another commitment and I can't make the home opener this Friday." He just stared at me. The seconds felt like minutes. He kept staring as if he was waiting for me to tell him I was kidding. I didn't dare tell him I was ditching to play with my band. We pledge allegiance to the team when we try out, and I was breaking that commitment. After another nauseating few moments, he coldly replied, "Do what you have to do."

And that was it.

My band went on to play the show. It was a packed house, a true taste of what was to come. After the show, I was on an emotional high. I couldn't believe what we had done. It was a dream come true and it felt incredible.

It wasn't long until I came crashing back to reality. My

inner critic had been right about one thing: I never started another game as a catcher. Coach gave my position to another player, and I couldn't blame him. My major league dream died that day, but where one dream ends, another begins.

There comes a time when you need to follow your heart and take a chance. It won't always feel good. You will doubt yourself. I did. I let it beat me up. My inner critic reminded me of my "mistake" all season. "You'll never start another game! You let your team down!" I let it cripple me. We made it to the playoffs that year, but got eliminated one game before the championship. I remember the lump in my throat when Coach looked at me one final time. "Suit up, kid, you're going in for the last inning." It was a mercy choice by him, to let me play the final three outs of my baseball career.

As I walked out of the dugout, my eyes filled with tears. This was it. The end of my time playing the game I loved, the end of a dream. I took my position behind home plate. I thought about how much I loved the game and how much I was going to miss it. I thought about the decision that had cost me my childhood dream. And then I thought about the concert. The crowd, the lights, the energy. I knew I'd made the right choice. I'd followed my heart.

I'm telling you this story because I want you to know it's okay to change your dream. As we journey through life, we change and our dreams can change. It's normal. Its okay. It's also okay to have negative chatter in your head. Listen to your heart, not your head. It will get you a lot farther in your life... and you'll be a lot happier.

Exercise: How To Listen To Your Inner Guidance

Do you ever wonder what people mean when they say, "follow your heart?" If you've ever found yourself wondering that, I want to clarify it for you. When I say "follow your heart," I don't mean that in the stereotypical sense you hear all the time. What I mean is, listen to your internal guidance.

Imagine you are presented with a difficult decision. Maybe it's about choosing to pursue one dream or to try another. Close your eyes and imagine yourself making one of these decisions. Let's call it Decision A. Think about how it feels having made that decision. Do you feel excited? Do you feel nervous?

Now I want you to shift. I want you to imagine yourself making the other decision. Decision B. Think about it, really pretend you're there, already having made the decision. How does this one feel? Is it more exciting? Is it less nerve-wracking?

Notice what comes up. One decision will always feel different than the other. The key is to notice the difference. Keep in mind that excitement and nervousness are the same emotion, just filtered through a different perception. For example, I used to get super-nervous before I went on stage but the more I did it, the faster my nervousness turned to excitement. Excitement is nervousness with experience.

What makes you feel uncomfortable will also make you feel the most alive. So while one decision might bring up a lot of feelings, the other might be more of a comfort for you. Be aware of this. The one that gives you comfort is usually the safer of the two paths, but rarely the most fulfilling. Don't sell yourself short. Embrace your nervousness and turn it into excitement.

Questions to ask yourself:

- Have you ever been faced with a tough decision and didn't know what to do?
- What does your inner critic tell you on a regular basis?
- Identify your negative chatter when it comes up and write it down. Do the *Finding My Dream* exercise and let it become a force that guides you.

16

DON'T BELIEVE EVERYTHING THAT YOU THINK

WHEN WE'RE FIRST STARTING OUT, our inner critic can seem like a stereo with the volume cranked to eleven, shooting us down, paralyzing our creative process. Forget the haters and trolls, that voice in our head can be the worst enemy of all, and it's a foe we all must face. It's the fear we must overcome, the doubt we must grow through. But just because our inner critic is trying to stop us, doesn't mean it's not serving a higher purpose. It's testing us to make us better, challenging us to see if we're truly ready to change—to prove we're committed.

If you find your mind getting the best of you try to observe the negative chatter. Is it true? When we speak, we create, and what we think, we tend to believe. But believing our thoughts all the time can get us into trouble. *Don't believe everything you think!* Often times, what we think simply isn't true and we waste energy dwelling on a made-up negative reality. One that doesn't serve us. Can you think of a time you beat yourself up thinking about something over and over only to find out it wasn't even true?

I still catch myself doing this. I'll be worried about a

made-up scenario in my head and stress myself out. When this happens, I've found it helpful to ask myself, "Is what I'm thinking the truth? Is it real?"

A while back, my band was prepping for a tour and I was late to rehearsal. I was running around my house trying to do a million things at once: packing, making breakfast, and getting everything in order because I'd be gone over a month. I rushed to the studio worried I was going to miss out on valuable rehearsal time. The more I thought about it, the more stressed I became. I thought, *I have to get there! Everyone is waiting on me...* When I got there, I hurried into the studio, only to learn the rest of my band was even later than me!

We tend to make up a version of reality that stresses us out. It's like our mind wants to mess with us. Questioning our thoughts helps us release the attachment and stress that comes from negative thinking. I'll share a technique to do that later in this chapter. But before we get to that, let's go deeper. Whenever negativity creeps up, ask yourself, "What can I do?"

Is what you're saying true? Is it necessary? Is it serving a higher purpose? I'm willing to bet its not. Ask these questions before you give your thoughts power over your life. This helps us notice how ridiculous our negative thoughts can be. You might even laugh them off because you realize their absurdity, but either way, take action.

Physical action works great too if you're stuck in a mental rut: go for a run, take a yoga class, workout, choose to get your body moving. Exercise is known to help mental health. It helps reduce things like anxiety and depression while improving self-esteem and how well our brain works. So if you're feeling stuck, take action! The mind and body function together as one; getting everything moving can help free ourselves from negativity.

———

WHEN WE SAY negative things in our head, it becomes increasingly easier to say negative things about other people. That's because our external world is a reflection of our internal world. If we think negative thoughts about ourselves then we look to express ourselves from a place of hurt without knowing we are hurt. So we take it out on other people. This isn't just a product of negative thinking, but of insecurity and conditioning.

If you find yourself engaging in negative gossip or some other form of judgmental expression, do what we did above, question it. Ask, "Is it real? Is it the truth? Is it serving a higher purpose?" How we treat (and talk about) others is a reflection of our internal dialogue and the relationship we have with ourselves.

We're all connected. So casting judgement on others is just like casting judgement on ourselves. If you hurt someone, you also hurt yourself. It will always be easier to gossip and judge others when we have negative inner chatter. If this happens, it means we need to expand and become aware of what's going on on an internal level. And if you're wondering why it's easy to engage in negative thought forms and harder to get out of them, it's because they're like quicksand; once you engage, it's easy to start sinking. It becomes effortless to stay where you are and keep sinking. It takes a lot more effort to climb out, stand up, and walk away.

In a subconscious way, we just want to connect, to be seen, heard and appreciated. But if we have some stuff in our head telling us things like, "I'm not good enough, I'm not cool enough, I'm not pretty enough." Then it's easier to bring others down with us, or at least try to.

There is a way to move past negativity. But in order to do that, we need to cultivate the awareness we've been talking about. Awareness that what we say and what we do to others will come back to us in one form or another. That's why it's important we treat others with the same respect we wish to receive ourselves.

Be aware. Awareness changes things.

———

BEFORE I KNEW I could control my thoughts I would let them beat me up. I didn't know I had the ability to step back and observe them. Once I discovered this power of bringing my awareness to my thoughts and to myself, I began watching my thoughts from another perspective. I found that many of them did not serve me. That was when I began the process of becoming aware, observing and then detaching from them.

Try this: Get into a quiet, comfortable place where you won't be disturbed. Close your eyes. Bring your awareness to that ruthless inner critic in your head. Listen to it. What is it telling you? Whatever it is, observe it. One way to do that is to imagine you're in a movie theater. Your thoughts are the movie playing on the screen and you're the projectionist. You get to choose what's playing. As you watch from behind the projector, you're not only seeing the movie, but seeing yourself *in* the movie. Just observe what's on the screen. Watch it. Watch what comes up. Do you like what you see? You get to choose what's playing, so if you don't like it, you can change it. You have that power.

Witness yourself, witness your thoughts, and witness your power in creating them.

You're much greater than you think, so be aware of the self-talk you engage in. Practicing this technique helps realize when unwanted past conditioning comes up, whether that's writing a book, going on stage, or trying anything new for the first time. When negative thoughts appear, notice them and remember your power to change them.

Be aware of your thoughts.

Awareness sets us free.

Questions to ask yourself:

- Can you remember a time you beat yourself up thinking about something over and over only to find out it wasn't true?
- Ask yourself, "Is what I'm thinking the truth? Is it even real?"
- Pretend you're watching your life as a movie. You see yourself and you see your thoughts up on the screen. Do you like what is playing?

PART IV

RELATIONSHIPS AND REALIZATIONS

WHAT VALUES embody a good relationship? I believe there are three: trust, communication, and acceptance. We develop trust by staying true to our word. We communicate by being open and honest. Finally, we create acceptance by not judging and doing our best to understand. Understanding happens when we listen to others with the intention to understand rather than to respond. It means asking questions to learn about the other person and their perspective because we genuinely want to understand them. The people in my life that I have developed the deepest relationships with are built on these three values—values that stand the test of time.

I am where I am in my life because of my relationships: my relationships with my band, my friends, my family. The more I invest in others and show up for them, the more my life transforms. It's not something you just do in the beginning, then slack off on. Establishing and maintaining healthy, long-term relationships are the building blocks of success.

When I realized the power of this, I was living in a tiny apartment in Anaheim, CA. It was fine for what it was, but the occasional gunshots and late night street racing kept me on edge. Around that time, I began making frequent trips to L.A.'s westside. I'd met a group of friends that I loved being around; they were artists, painters, chefs, musicians—all kinds of creative types. They accepted me and saw me as someone greater than I saw myself at the time, and it felt fantastic. I was living an hour away, but was up there four or five times a week.

For the longest time, my westside friends thought I lived nearby. They would compliment me on my punctuality because I made a point to arrive on-time to every event and get-together. When my friends learned how far I was driving to see them, they were blown away! But I didn't think anything of it. It was all part of establishing trust and good communication. The relationships I developed with them became the catalyst for my personal transformation through self-expression, art, dance, and creativity in general. Since I started hanging out with them, my life has never been the same.

Not long after, one of them invited me to be their room-mate at a beach house in Malibu. I went from hearing gunshots and street racing every night to nothing but calm ocean waves. That's the power of surrounding yourself with positive, supportive people. They find all kinds of ways to change your life for the better.

That goes for my band as well. I grew up with them; we're legit brothers. And if it wasn't for the relationships I forged with them, I wouldn't be in one of the biggest independent bands on the planet. So find positive people who share similar interests and goals. People you can count on and who can count on you. These are the ones who see the best in you when you can't see it in yourself. Finding them and forging those connections will do wonders for your career and personal growth.

Sometimes that takes noticing other people's gifts and supporting them, like we mentioned earlier. When you support others and celebrate them, then more comes back to you.

It all starts with relationships. So how can we build positive ones? Stay true to what you say. We all know people who will say one thing and do another, or who will give their word and then not follow through. Stuff comes up, things happen, but the value of our word is the most valuable currency we have. It takes effort to develop and maintain its value. That means staying true to your word, and making sure your words align with your actions. If you say you'll do something, do it! If you commit to an event, show up. Be present. By doing so, you embody trust, communication, and acceptance—exactly the kind of person we all want in our lives. This applies to friends, lovers, employers, everyone.

Because not enough people demonstrate these values, that means when you do, it becomes the easiest way for you to stand out and get noticed. People naturally want to help the people who help them. It creates a positive feedback loop where everyone benefits, and everyone rises. We can only get so far on our own, so strive to build positive relationships. They will change your life!

17

ONE MILLION FOLLOWERS

THE GOLDEN RULE STATES, "Treat others the way you wish to be treated." Simple enough, right? Well, I had no idea its power when I was a kid. At the time I thought it was lame, just another one of those things parents insist we do. I didn't realize until much later in life how powerful this rule is.

Why is it so powerful? Treating people the way we wish to be treated helps us unlock potential opportunities and relationships. It helps us be the kind of person other people want to be around. It also sets an example of how we wish to be treated. When we hold other people in a higher regard, one that feels good for them and for us, it allows them to be themselves, because they aren't being judged. Without judgement, we find acceptance. Continued acceptance helps develop trust, one of the most important principles in developing solid relationships.

Everyone is a reflection of you. This "golden rule" is magical because it gives others a glimpse into how you see them—and how you see yourself. When this is positive, people enjoy our presence more. When people enjoy our presence, they want to be around us. And when people want to be around us, we have more opportunities to develop a stronger relationship with them.

Unfortunately, thanks to social media, we seem to be forgetting this idea. More than ever, we seem to be willing to place our self-worth in the number of our followers instead of in real friendships.

We've all seen it: People treating others differently based on their social media following. Conversations that seem low energy at first suddenly light up when we find out the other person has a large following. Then it's as if something has changed, that the other person is suddenly cooler, more attractive, and way more interesting. Did anything really change? No! But our perspective did.

Throughout human history, we've always seen value in the traditional institutions of money and power, but we're just now evolving with technology to add social media into the mix. These are all great resources that help us live our dream, but they aren't the definition of our worth as people. How we treat ourselves and how we treat others is the true definition of what makes us a success. The rest of it— anything that doesn't come from within—is secondary. Maybe that seems difficult because of the way society has brought us up, but it doesn't have to be. There's an easy way to do it, and that's simply to treat everyone like they have a million followers.

Now ask yourself, what if you treated everyone like that?

- Would you see them as more valuable?
- Would you treat them any different?

If you experiment with this mindset, you may start to notice...

You're open to more opportunities. By treating others

well, you create an opening for new experiences as well as potential opportunities. You never know who you could meet, who you could help, or what valuable information someone might share. This can lead to amazing advice or even life-long connections. However, if you remain closed off, not seeing the value in others, you shut yourself off from opportunity.

People seem more attractive. That's because you're seeing others not only as reflections of who you are, but as fellow rock stars. When this happens, acknowledge it. You might find it easier to hold conversation. You might feel more inclined to smile or say hello. You might notice beauty in others you didn't see before. You're noticing the awesomeness that is in you and it is being reflected in others. Keep in mind I don't mean sexually attractive; I mean attractive in a general sense, as in someone who it feels good to be around.

You're More Confident. How we treat others is a reflection of how we treat ourselves. By seeing others as having value, we begin to see the value we bring. Everyone is going through struggles—things we have no idea about. Having a positive reaction to them can be a game-changer. It can lift them up right when they need it most and create an experience they may never forget.

For the longest time, I struggled with seeing my value. I thought because I was around extremely gifted musicians I could never be on their level. It hurt. It made me feel like every question I asked was stupid, that I should already know the answer. I beat myself up for years and held my tongue in situations where I could have learned a lot more by asking questions. Back then, I didn't see myself the way the world saw me. People saw me as the bass player in a successful band, yet I didn't identify as a "real" musician, let alone a successful one. I was constantly worried people might learn I wasn't good enough.

Fortunately, it was all in my head. I hadn't developed the confidence to just go for it, to stop giving a shit what other people think. That all changed when I started hanging out with people who saw my value and put me in the position to grow. They introduced me to others as an "amazing musician." You don't know how many times I wanted to correct them, to insist I wasn't that good, but I stopped myself because I didn't want to embarrass them. I just shook hands and smiled awkwardly, wondering when everyone would figure out it was all a lie...

But you know what? The more my friends insisted I was amazing, the more it made me wonder, maybe they were right and I was being too hard on myself. So I sat with the idea for a while, this image others had of me as an "amazing musician." These were smart people. They couldn't all be wrong, so why was I fighting it? I began telling myself they were right, I was amazing, and that made all the difference. And this is what happened as a result: I began stepping up and playing with people I didn't normally play with. I surrendered the idea of who I thought I was for the image of something greater. I became okay with messing up and embracing my newfound confidence. It didn't matter if I failed, I would figure it out and keep going.

Sometimes it takes others seeing something we don't in order to believe it ourselves. This is why relationships are so valuable. The insights they offer are what give us the opportunity to see what they see in us, and for us to see the value in them. That's why treating others like they have a million followers is so powerful. Because you're treating yourself as the person of value, and in turn, seeing the value others bring. Doing this creates stronger, more powerful relationships with everyone you meet.

When I say, "Treat everyone like they have a million followers," I don't mean putting people on a pedestal. Not at all. I simply mean we're seeing the value in every person, in every moment. We're treating them the way we want to be treated. We have a tendency to glorify people who are successful or famous. This can be stressful, causing us to think we're not good enough and we need to worship the ground they walk on. Screw that! We're all human, and that's what this million followers idea gets to the heart of: See others as you see yourself, but also treat others with the same respect, love, and openness you wish to receive. We're not glamorizing others when we do this, we're increasing our ability to see value, both in ourselves and others. In doing so, we not only lift others, we lift ourselves. So try it out for a day and treat everyone like they have a million followers. See how it feels.

Questions to ask yourself:

- Would you treat people different if they had a million followers?
- Would you treat yourself different if you had a million followers?
- Experiment for a day and treat everyone as if they we're a reflection of you; how would you want to be treated?

18

DEALING WITH NEGATIVITY

MAYBE YOU'RE on the path to change, but still encountering negativity. If the source of negative talk is coming from the people you spend the most time with, then it's possible they're going through similar issues we talked about in chapter 3: Dealing With Haters and Trolls. That's okay, we now know that we have the power to change our thinking through awareness and observation. But, no matter how good we get at keeping our self-talk positive, we'll still run into negative people. Sadly, they're everywhere. Dealing with them can be discouraging, especially when they're the people closest to us. So what can we do?

Life is going to throw you curveballs. Remember how our tour bus driver robbed us of $20k? We thought we were going to make a lot of money that tour, only to barely end up breaking even. Shit happens. Trying to avoid negative people in life only avoids opportunity. In some weird, sadistic way, negative people make us stronger because we get to figure out how to keep our energy up around them. I'm not saying it's easy, but what we need to learn seems to find us, regardless of whether we try to avoid it. So don't run. Don't hide. Frame it as a learning experience.

Everyone's brain is wired to manipulate others to attract attention. It has everything to do with how we were raised. We were conditioned by our need to receive attention when we were little. This was dependant upon our parents or the people who raised us. It's a survival instinct. As kids, we need attention from adults to develop properly. Over the course of our development, we learn subconscious ways of getting other people to pay attention to us.

Some get angry, aggressive, or demanding of others. Some get quiet. Some pretend they don't understand. Others turn into victims. These are all ways of trying to gain attention in order to feel better about ourselves. It's a way of trying to feel more important and more complete. When we're little, we don't know how to give ourselves the attention we need to feel good, so we rely on others. Unfortunately, many people don't learn how to do this in adulthood either, so we find ourselves living in a world with others who, without awareness, manipulate others to feel good. They keep trying to fill themselves up this way, but it's a shortcut. It never lasts. They're like boats with holes in the bottom, forever in need of attention.

There's a better way. First, understand that meeting others with the same negative emotion they're projecting only makes things worse. What I mean is, if someone is aggressive and you meet them with aggression, it's like throwing gasoline on a fire. Somewhere along the line, they learned if they get pissed, others will pay attention. If you get pissed, it's now a contest to see who's going to get more angry. I'm not saying to go the other way, because playing the victim feeds the fire through submission. Instead of being angry or falling into a victim mentality, call it out.

Remember, awareness changes things! Saying to someone, "I notice that you seem angry; how can I help?" or "How you're speaking to me is stressing me out; could we try talking about this in a different way?" brings the other person's awareness to what is going on and that you want to help them reach a positive outcome for both of you. Don't use a condescending tone, that will only make things worse. *You have to be sincere.* It becomes harder for someone to continue a behavior the moment you call it out, but it needs to come from a non-emotional place. When you put it that way, the other person has no choice but to notice it. Whether they continue to act that way isn't your problem if you aren't feeding into it.

If someone is playing the victim instead of being angry, we can help them reframe it by telling them the good we see in them. Or asking why they feel the way they do. Feelings are funky things, we can't touch them and we can't see them, but they're real. When we bring our focus to them through awareness and reframing, they can be changed for the better.

Now I want to talk to you about the people in your life—specifically what to do if they insist on being negative despite your best efforts. It may not be their time to shift into a positive mindset. We can't force anyone to change.

Friends and family can hold us back if they're not willing to change and grow with us. Not necessarily to go after the same things in life, but in the same positive direction. When that happens, when you know certain people are holding you back, then you may need to limit your time with them or, in extreme cases, cut them out of your life entirely.

People come into our lives for a reason, and they also go

out for a reason. Sometimes they come to support us, some-times for us to support them. Sometimes, they come to test us. But in the end, the most important relationship is your relationship with yourself. It's the longest-term one you have. If others don't want to grow with you, it's okay. We're all on our own path.

If you're still wondering if you should distance yourself with someone, consider how that person makes you feel. If the positive outweighs the negative, then keep them around, but dial it back a bit. Instead of hanging out everyday, limit your time with them. In extreme cases, you might need to take an extended vacation from them.

Understand that cutting people off doesn't mean they will be out of your life forever... you're just making yourself a priority. Maybe that will inspire them to do the same, but remember you can't make someone change, they have to want it for themselves. Maybe once they see your commit-ment to change and positivity, they will want to work through whatever is holding them back. But that's not your job. Think about it this way: By showing them the success that positive change brings, you'll do more to help them than you ever could by holding yourself back.

Questions to ask yourself:

- In what ways do you tend to react to others? Do you get angry, shy, or sad? Take note of it. You can change by expressing yourself positively and asking questions.
- Are there people in your life that bring you down?

- Could you manage your time better? Maybe spend less time with them and more with other, more positive people?

19

ROCK AND ROLL LEGEND

Vans Warped Tour was the tour of all tours in the punk, rock, and alternative scene. A summer-long festival across the US. It embraced all types of music, hosting artists like Blink 182, Eminem, and Katy Perry (just to name a few). It was the holy grail of tours for our band and growing up, we dreamed to play it.

Back in 2015, over a decade after we formed Our Last Night, we found out we got it and it meant the world to us. In order to give back to the Warped community, I decided to host restorative yoga classes each night for the bands, roadies, and tour staff. It was something special to help us chill out and detox the stress of working in the summer heat. I figured it would be fun and I'd get to connect with new people in deep and meaningful ways.

Through my classes, I developed a strong friendship with a woman named Shelleylyn. She owns the company that catered the tour and was in charge of feeding over 800 people. After attending a few of my yoga classes, she confessed that what I was doing meant a lot to her. Shelleylyn was going through a difficult break-up, along with the hectic nature of feeding the tour three times a day. She really needed to let go of the stress and clear her mind.

One evening, Shelleylyn came up to me and said her friend was coming to the tour in a few days and she would love to introduce me to him. I didn't think anything of it other than saying I'd be happy to meet him.

The day arrived. After I ate lunch, I saw Shelleylyn at the catering area, and she told me that her friend, Gene, was on his way and she needed someone to hang with him because she'd be busy preparing the dinner service.

Now at this point, I was a little curious. So I asked, "Gene who?" and she replied, "Gene Simmons." I almost spit out my drink! When I got control of myself, I said, "You mean you're friends with Gene Simmons? From KISS? *That* Gene Simmons?" And she said, "Yup."

My mind was blown. Here I was on my first major festival tour, and now I was being asked to not just hang with a true rock and roll legend, but to be his guide for the afternoon!

An hour later, Shelleylyn texted me he'd arrived.

I'll never forget walking around the tour with a legitimate rock and roll legend. I felt like a total boss. Grown men who I had been on tour with all summer were running up to him like fanboys asking for pictures and autographs. And here I was, kicking it with Gene Simmons.

What struck me most about Gene was his demeanor. Calm and collected, but never really serious. I would imagine that being in an iconic rock band like KISS would generate some sort of entitlement, but he seemed nonchalant and casual. Of course, he didn't need to act big time, *he was big time (and still is).*

We sat in the catering area for dinner. The dinner conversation consisted of Gene asking about my band and what we sounded like. I told him our closest reference was Linkin Park, to which he asked if we played "real" instruments or if we did that "fake" electronic stuff. I told him we did play our instruments but we also did have sample tracks. He wasn't impressed. "None of that fake stuff," he complained. "You have to actually play your music."

I remember feeling doubt come into my mind as if we weren't good enough. I let Gene know we didn't have a record label and had been making a living through online streaming, digital sales, and YouTube. That got his attention, so I explained how we'd built our business model off of the hip-hop world of mixtapes, but instead of mixtapes, we did covers of songs that helped grow our fanbase, and brought awareness to our original material. He looked at me in wonder, and I could tell it made him think a bit. Whether he gained a newfound respect for me or not, I have no idea, but he did admit, "The world is certainly changing..." to which he added, "but you still have to play your instruments."

I understand what Gene meant. He's been outspoken in the media about his belief that rock and roll is dead, which makes sense hearing a lot of modern music and how the music is moving more digital. Rock, especially from an old school perspective, is about giving it your all, being real and raw, however that looks for you. For some, it might be face paint, for others it might be jumping around on stage. I took it as him saying to be real. *Be yourself. Don't try to be something you're not.* And when it comes down to relationships, I think a lot of people don't know how to be real. It's not our fault. We're all caught up judging ourselves based on how we compare to other people's success. So how can we keep it real?

Invest in others.

What does that mean? It means showing up for other

people and building relationships. On that Warped Tour, I connected with Shelleylyn because I wanted to give back. I wanted to serve and I showed up consistently. When we do this, we create relationships that are stronger than superficial small talk. When we invest in people by asking ourselves, "How can I serve?" we create a deeper experience. One that expands our mind to places we never thought possible, like hanging with Gene Simmons.

When you serve from love and a desire to help, then your life transforms through the relationships you build. So ask yourself, "How Can I Serve?" Act on what comes up and watch what happens. I'm not saying you'll spend the day with Gene Simmons, but I'm not saying you won't. Cool things will happen, and they'll keep happening.

Questions to ask yourself:

- In what ways could you show up to support others?
- What could you do to add value to others?
- Ask yourself, "How can I serve?"

20

LOVE AND FEAR

HAVE YOU EVER BEEN in a relationship you knew wasn't going to work out? Most of us have, in one form or another. So why do we stay in them? Usually it's because of fear—the fear of being alone, the fear of the unknown, or what other people will think if we fail.

For example, years ago, I was afraid my girlfriend would break up with me and I'd never find someone as special as her. I stayed in the relationship out of fear, not love, and this bad decision spilled over into every area of life—especially with my band. Even when I was with them, I wasn't really with them. I wasn't present, in the moment, giving them my best. I couldn't because my thoughts kept drifting back to worrying about my relationship.

When I would go on tour, I would wish I was home with her. You know, so I could help make sure she was happy. And when I came home, it was great. We'd have our honeymoon phase, but it would only last about a week. After that, I wished I was back on tour, away from her and the issues in our relationship. This was the cycle for two years, with me constantly wishing I was somewhere I wasn't. It was a mess, and it almost cost me my dream.

Fortunately, she broke up with me before that could happen. Why did she do it? Because fear isn't attractive, and she could sense mine. There was no way I could hide it. But the main reason, the one I want you to focus on, is that what we fear, we create. Not always in the way we expect, but in some form or another. We make it happen by giving it our focus and our energy. Without meaning to, we attract what we don't want by thinking about it. Similar to how we attract what we do want.

I don't blame my ex-. I wasn't clear with what I wanted from our relationship, so there was no way it could be successful. If I had, maybe I could have found a way to balance my commitment to her with my commitment to the band. But I let fear get in the way, and once you let fear in, it messes things up. No relationship is perfect, but even at its worst, your reason to stay should be motivated by love, not fear.

One of the main reasons we stay in unhealthy relationships is because we think we can change the other person. It's easy to fall into the trap of waiting around, hoping the other person will change. It's even easier to think we can change them. Have you ever done that? Full transparency, most of the relationships I've had in my life I've seen red flags and thought, "It's okay, they'll change, or I can change them." Has it ever worked? NO! We can't change anyone. They have to change themselves. It's not healthy to think we can do it. We can support them and show our love, but the source of change has to come from within them, not from us. It can be inspired by something else, like a coach, counselor, or friend, but sadly, it never works when it comes from inside the relationship.

Back in the beginning of Part 2, I mentioned the "boat without a captain" analogy, and it definitely applies here. To recap, it said that without direction, we float aimlessly. When we think scattered, contradictory thoughts about what we want, it leads to confusion and lack of success. For me, it was with my band and my girlfriend. For you, it could be balancing pursuit of your dream against the responsibilities of your day job, your school, or your family. Whatever it is, the important thing is to stay balanced. Keep making progress, even if it seems small. Do your best and be open about what you would like from your relationships. This will help create the balance necessary to build healthy relationships while you go for your dream.

When we let fear be the root of our decision-making, we limit our potential. In the same way that staying in a relationship you know isn't healthy for you, making decisions about your dream based on fear limits your ability to achieve them. When it comes down to it, we all make decisions out of love or fear. So before you choose to act, ask yourself, "Is this a decision based on love or fear?" Knowing the difference will guide you toward a healthy balance.

Before we end this chapter, I need to clarify one thing: Success isn't about having one area in your life that's good while the rest suck. If you have a ton of money, but your relationships are awful, that's not success. If you have a successful job but you're not happy, that's not success either. You deserve success in every area of life. Some will say, "You have to sacrifice for success." I call bullshit on that. You have to learn to *balance*.

We want to be clear on what our dream is and how to achieve it, like we did in the *Finding My Dream* exercise, but we also need to balance our life in healthy ways. How we do this is by choosing love over fear and communicating honestly. That means being clear with ourselves and others while working toward success.

Questions to ask yourself:

- Have you ever stayed in a relationship or friendship thinking the other person would change? What was the outcome?
- Are you choosing love or fear?
- Do you strive for well-rounded success? Identify one area of your life you could give more love to, then do it.

21

CHOOSE ONE (YOU CAN'T HAVE BOTH)

THERE'S ONE DAY that stands out in my mind when it comes to making choices. It was summer 2007. Everything in my life was clicking into place. We were driving to a show and our manager at the time was riding with us. He'd helped sign us to Epitaph Records. Naturally, we all looked up to him. He'd taken us to the next level. However, on that day, my excitement shifted to nervousness. Mid-drive, he looked me dead in the eyes and said, "You can't be in the band and do school, Woody. You gotta choose one."

At the time, I was about to go into my junior year at the University of New Hampshire. I didn't really know exactly what I wanted to do with my degree, but I did know that it was important to finish what I started—that meant both school and the band.

Back in the van, my stomach was in knots, my palms sweaty. Was this what they meant by "New Level, New Devil?" Surely my manager wasn't the Devil, but what he said challenged me. Did he have any business telling me what I could or couldn't do outside the band? Was he entitled to tell me how to live because he helped get us signed? I didn't know if I should believe him or not.

Sometimes, we run into people who think they know what's best for us. Remember, most people are speaking from their experience, but if they are coming from a limited mindset, they might not be able to see your commitment and drive to make it happen. So if you have someone tell you you can't do something, think about it. Can you use it as motivation? Can you put a chip on your shoulder and go after what you want with such perseverance and passion that it will leave them scratching their heads wondering, "How the hell did they do that?"

In that moment in our van, after being told I couldn't be in my band and finish school, I felt a shift happen. I was still feeling anxious and unsure, but this was the challenge the universe was presenting me with. In my head, I knew he was just the messenger. All I could think about was, "Oh yeah? Watch me."

I kept that chip on my shoulder and every time it got tough, I remembered that manager's words. That edge helped me do things I wouldn't normally do, like meeting with my professors one-on-one to let them know I was willing to do whatever it took to pass their classes *and* pursue my dream.

And I did graduate. It took a lot of work, a lot of communication, and a lot of courage. But when we know what we want, we're more likely to find others who can help get us there. We just have to be clear and willing to put in the effort. Not every band would have understood, but I'm not in any band, I'm in a band with my childhood best friends. They were super-supportive because I was clear and told them what I wanted: to be in the band and finish school. That made all the difference.

My point is, use other's doubt as motivation. If someone tells you how to live and you don't agree, look at it as a challenge to step up your game. Let it fuel your fire. Here's a powerful example... Most people who aren't New England Patriots fans throw shade at Tom Brady. I get it, people who win are easy to hate. But did you know he was drafted as the 199th pick in the NFL draft? He had scouts saying he was too slow, lacked arm strength, and even the ability to be an NFL quarterback. Now he's one of the greatest if not *the* greatest quarterbacks to ever play the game. But still, he's never let that go. He uses it as motivation. And that's what I want you to do. When someone challenges you or says it's impossible to get what you want or to do what you wish, let that be your fire. Prove them wrong. Not for revenge—this isn't about them, it's about you and proving to yourself what you can do.

Which reminds me... After I graduated, I saw our manager again—except this time, he wasn't our manager. A while back, he'd told us he wasn't into it anymore. There were no hard feelings, he was honest with us, and we appreciated everything he'd done, but that didn't stop me from telling him I'd just graduated and was still in the band. It felt great, and in a way, it almost felt like thanking him for lighting that fire in me.

MAYBE YOU'RE WORRIED that the people who doubt you are right, or maybe you think you don't have time to pursue your dream and everything else. I get it, life is complicated. It's easy to get distracted, to get sidetracked by doubt. When that happens, do your best to just keep going. Handle what you need to do and get back on track with your goals.

Do something to move you toward your dream every day. Even if it's just one quick little thing. It could be a social media post, or writing a few paragraphs on your novel, or practicing your instrument, reading a book, or taking an online course... Just do something, even if it's just five minutes. Whatever you can make time for, just make the time! So many of us blame not having enough time for not being able to get what we want. We all have the same number of hours in the day, the same number of days in the week. We don't have a time issue, we have a priority issue.

What separates us from being a rock star or not is how we prioritize our time. Maybe that means you get up an hour earlier, or go to bed an hour later. Maybe you skip watching TV or playing video games until you get something done to move you closer to your dream. Prioritize the things that create momentum. Prioritize what keeps you moving—both towards what you wish to create and how you want to live.

Keep track of your progress in a journal or notepad; this provides real tangible proof that you are creating progress because you can see it. Once you see it, you can analyze it and ask yourself, "Am I closer to my dream than if I'd spent those hours on something else?" Review your progress at regular intervals; that could mean daily, weekly, or monthly.

Taking positive action each day, no matter how small, is how you generate the momentum to reach your goals. It's also a great way to feel good about yourself because progress creates happiness.

Taking positive daily action, no matter how small, is great for morale. Consistency is the key. That's how we build lifestyle shifts on a rock star level. Keeping track of your progress each day in a journal or note pad provides real, tangible proof that you're clear on what you want, and making time for it.

Questions to ask yourself:

- Has someone ever doubted you? Did they try to impose their beliefs on you? Did you use it as motivation to succeed? Can you now?
- If someone tells you how to live and you don't agree, can you choose to look at it as a challenge to step up your game?
- How do you prioritize your time? Is there a better way you could balance where you give your energy to make your dreams closer to reality?

22

MONEY

To be successful, we need to change our relationship not just with ourselves, not just with others, but with everything —especially money. Money is the most misunderstood thing in many people's lives and if you don't understand what money is really for, you'll never be happy no matter how much you make.

Maybe you think that when you reach a certain status or income bracket, you won't feel fear, won't feel doubt. No matter who you are or how far you've risen, we're still human. Doubt and fear are hardwired into us. Just because we get the perfect job, perfect relationship, or perfect income doesn't mean the doubt and fear goes away.

Why do you think so many rich people seem so unhappy? Because they've been so busy focused on their external world that they forgot to work on what's most important: their inner world. What I mean by that is yes, you want your external world to be awesome and abundant. There's nothing wrong with being rich, but the best way to achieve that goal is to focus on your inner world first.

Your inner world lays the foundation you build your

dream house on. It has to be solid, rock solid, or else external factors can come along and blow your house down. In other words, money alone can't make you happy. Neither can fame or love or anything that comes from outside yourself. Sure, it might provide the illusion that you're happy because you're filled with endorphins and riding that high, but it will wear off. Then you'll want more, and chasing that emotional high becomes a constant quest for something unattainable. Don't fall into the trap!

Only you can make yourself happy. That's important—so important, I'm going to say it again: *Only you can make yourself happy.*

External happiness comes and goes. You can't control it because there are too many variables. But internal happiness has the longevity to stay with you for your entire life. That's because peace and calm come from being truly happy, and self-reflection reminds us what's actually important: the peace within. Once you're happy being who you are, you'll know what to do with success when it comes (and it will).

Maybe you're doubting what I say is true. Maybe you think money really can buy happiness. That's an easy mistake to make, especially in our consumer-driven, capitalist society. The media is constantly selling us on the idea that if only we had more money, we could have the "perfect life." So naturally, money is going to be first and foremost on our minds—at least in the beginning. And to be honest, up to a certain amount, money does instill peace of mind. Constantly needing to worry about meeting basic needs like paying rent can be tough. But after that, money and happiness take two different turns...

Maybe you bought this book because that's what you thought you needed: more money. And you do, we all do, up to a point, but the thing we need to learn is money can't buy happiness. What money really does—and I mean money in its purest, most powerful sense—is it gives us freedom.

Money is freedom.

Say it with me: *Money is freedom.*

It's not about being rich. Being rich just to be rich is a terrible idea because it's greed without purpose. No, being rich is about what money lets you do to enhance your life and the lives of others. It gives you options. It gives you freedom. So the first thing we need to do is change our relationship with money if we're ever going to enjoy success.

I'm going to tell you a story now, and I know it will seem trivial at first. On the surface, it is. But underneath, on the inside, it hurt me. It hurt me so bad it served as a wake up call.

A few years out of college, I was food shopping on a tight budget. I remember standing in the supermarket aisle weighing the cost of organic almond milk versus regular almond milk. I know, total first world problems. But bear with me, there's an important lesson here. I told myself I couldn't afford organic. But my inner critic didn't just tell me I couldn't afford it, oh no... Do you know what it told me?

That I didn't deserve it.

That hurt, and was totally untrue. I deserve to be healthy. We all do. How healthy we can afford to be on our current budgets is a matter for debate, but it's no reason to beat ourselves up.

During this time in my life, I was living paycheck to paycheck, not sure I could pay my bills and still make rent. I felt uncertain and small. So I lived that way, not knowing that by doing so, I was creating more of what I didn't want in my life. I was telling myself I couldn't do this, couldn't do that, that I wasn't worthy or good enough to get what I wanted. *That I didn't deserve it.* And the worst part was I thought I was thinking positive!

That night driving home from the grocery store, I had my phone playing YouTube videos: motivational speakers I enjoy listening to. But none of it was sinking in. I was too mad at myself. My inner critic's constant echo insisting I didn't deserve what I wanted really got under my skin. It wasn't about the almond milk. It was deeper than that. The almond milk was just a symbol—a symbol for everything that was wrong in my life.

As my inner critic continued to insult me, it literally brought me to tears. I was frustrated and pissed off because I'd let this negative voice control how I felt about myself. How was I supposed to be a rock star with this damn voice telling me it would never happen?

So you know what I did? I screamed, "Shut up! Just shut the hell up!" Over and over on the drive home, I told my inner critic off, and I did it as loud as I could. I was sick and tired of wanting more and not getting it. I yelled louder and louder until I drowned out the negative voice in my head and even the sound of the video from my phone. Then, as if from a higher power, my phone switched to the next video on a random playlist.

The perfect video. The one I needed to hear.

It came on, and as I drove, I heard a man named Justin Perry talk about how he went from making minimum wage to a million dollars a year. I stopped shouting. My ears perked up. Justin gave five affirmations he said to read every day, and not just once, but multiple times. He said this would change my internal dialogue about money and in turn, about me. It made sense. It felt right. I decided to listen to him and fight my inner critic by taking positive action —*positive reinforcement*. To do that, I had to change my internal dialogue. I had to change my relationship with money to convince myself I not only deserved that damned almond milk, but everything else I was working toward.

The first thing I did when I got home was to write down the five affirmations Justin told me about. I read them out loud over and over in the mirror. At first, it was difficult and I didn't believe it. But after putting more conviction in my voice, I started to feel good. *Really good.* I puffed my chest out and stood taller. I spoke with intention, as if my words were already true. I spoke them as if they were my destiny. For the first time in my life, I was aware of the feeling of abundance. It came over me like a glow. I knew I was on to something powerful. Something that had the power to change my life forever.

I'll share these affirmations with you now. Feel free to use them "as is" or adapt them to your needs. Like all affirmations, make sure they are written in the present tense and 100% positive.

Five Daily Affirmations to Build Wealth

1. I always have enough money to share and to spare.
2. Every day in every way, my wealth is increasing.
3. Money comes to me easily and effortlessly.
4. I have more money than I know what to do with.
5. My income is constantly increasing.

— Justin Perry, "How to Be a Money Magnet"

I said these affirmations every day, multiple times, just like Justin told me to. A year later, my life was unrecognizable. My bank account and new friendships were abundant, all because I changed my thinking. Specifically, I changed what I was focusing on, from negative to positive.

Even now, years later, I continue to say these affirmations out loud. I do it in my meditation practice as well as in the mirror. I do it whenever I feel my inner critic return.

Because I deserve to be happy and successful.

I deserve to live my life and my dream.

And so do you.

Questions to ask yourself:

- When you think of money, what do you feel? Do you feel positive or abundant? Or do you feel anxious and stressed. Write down the five affirmations I mentioned and put them somewhere you'll see everyday. Read them out loud in the morning and at night. Can you do it for one week straight?
- Have you ever told yourself you didn't deserve what you wanted? How can you shift that mindset?
- Could you take a stand against your negative thinking? Would you be willing to stand up and tell your inner critic to shut up?

23

THE POWER OF WORDS

IMAGINE if other people could read your thoughts. Yeah WTF, I know. For sure, that would suck. Luckily for us, most people can't read our mind. Most people can, however, feel the vibrations of our words. You know that saying, "Sticks and stones can break my bones, but names will never hurt me"? Talk about a load of crap! If modern science has taught us anything, it's that everything vibrates at a frequency. Sticks, stones, and yes, our words.

Have you ever heard someone sing and their voice gave you chills? Maybe it made you emotional and you weren't sure why. Well, sound is a vibration and when we create sound using our words, we have the ability to impact people and ourselves, making our words a tool. Like any tool, words can be used for good or bad. Meaning yes, names can hurt us. Especially if we allow them to become a part of the story we tell ourselves.

In a weird, trippy way, our thoughts impact what we create in our life. Kind of like how if you don't think you're good enough to write a song you never try to, or if you do have a song but think it isn't good enough, you never release it. The words we speak to ourselves are all creations of what's in our head. If we don't think we're good enough, we will never get out of our way to try. Which means, what we think we become.

Can you think of a time when someone said something that stuck in your head? A time when you started to believe something about yourself just because someone else said it?

I had the pleasure of hearing Jim Kwik speak a few years ago. Jim's a consciousness hacker; he trains people to speed read, remember names, and increase cognitive ability, which is a fancy word for brain power. In a nutshell, Jim's a genius when it comes to learning. But in his speech, he told a story about how when he was a little kid, a teacher referred to him as "the boy with the broken brain." He carried this idea of having a "broken brain" with him throughout his childhood thinking he wasn't good enough. All because he allowed someone's else's beliefs to become his own.

Who says that kind of crap to an impressionable kid? Especially a teacher! That's crazy. On the other hand, I think it's amazing to see how what others say about us can impact us in such a powerful way. And if we can be aware of how it happens, then maybe we can choose what we let in, or even more, what we let go of. We might even start to question where all this crap in our head comes from, if it serves us, and if it's actually true. Chances are, if it's negative, it's not.

Take a moment and think about that. Get in a safe, quiet space, close your eyes, and think of a negative thought you have about yourself. Examine it closely. Where did it come from? Why do you believe it and allow it to stay? How has it shaped your life and held you back? It's time to transform that negative thought. It's time to replace it with its opposite, positive version. Make sure the new thought is present-tense and constructed as if it's already true. Say it out loud with a positive emotion tied to it. Remember attaching emotion to new thought will help bring it into existence. Think about how you feel being the rock star of your life. Is it exciting? Do you feel free? Do you feel liberated? Use these feelings in your new thought. Maybe something along the lines of "I feel free knowing I am enough," or "I am excited to know I am moving toward my goals." Choose the emotion you want to feel with your thought and say it out loud. Repeat it to yourself a few times.

How does it feel? Does the emotion you're tying it to feel impactful? You might find that it does, you also might want to make adjustments to your new thought, either in your words or emotion, go ahead and do it, then do it again if need be, make it feel good. Not everything feels the same for every person. You get to find out what works best for you. Feel free to experiment.

Once you have something you like, say it over and over until you feel it. *Really feel it.* The key is to create the belief by tying repetition with the new positive emotion. Don't be discouraged if you don't see results right away. Stick with it. It can take a while to reframe a belief that doesn't serve us. Especially if we've been believing it for a long time. So just like the money affirmations in Chapter 22, repeat this new thought to yourself every day. Set a goal to do it for a week, then maybe a month. If the older thought comes up, acknowledge it, then replace it with the positive by saying it in your head or out loud. Repeat this process with any negative thought you notice in your head. Write each of the replacement thoughts down and add them to your list of affirmations to say every day.

Questions to ask yourself:

- Has anyone ever said something negative to you that then became part of the story you tell yourself? Was it true?
- In what area of your life have you been holding yourself back?
- What would you say to yourself if you had already accomplished your goals and were living your dream?

24

STAY TRIPPY, STAY OPEN

HAVE YOU HEARD of quantum physics? Maybe you heard of it for the first time when you watched *Ant-Man* or *Avengers: Endgame*. The quantum world is pretty much everything shrunk to the proton/electron level. Now there's this wild experiment that scientists did to try and understand how matter behaves on a quantum level. Scientists fired electrons (a.k.a. matter) through two tiny slits and waited to see what happened on the other side. Instead of going through the two slits, the matter appeared to act like a wave, surprisingly not two lines but multiple lines of matter were found on the wall behind the slits. This made no sense as there should have only been two lines from the matter going through two slits.

To try and figure out what happened, the scientists decided to watch. They put a camera next to the slits to see what the matter was doing. When they did this, something even weirder happened. The matter went back to behaving the way they predicted and there ended up being only two lines on the back wall. Trippy, right? What they concluded was not only did the matter behave like a wave of potential but it "chose" to act different when it "knew" it was being watched. Meaning the act of observing collapsed the wave function... which is just a fancy way of saying, when you observe your world, you change the outcome of it.

So how does this apply to you being a rock star? Well, if the very act of observing matter (which makes up pretty much everything) changes how matter behaves, then isn't it possible to take control of what it is we create in our life? I think so.

Remember how we got clear about what we want in the *Finding My Dream* exercise? This is one of the major reasons why. The simple act of us observing what's going on in our lives—the positive and the negative—changes the outcome. Which is a way of saying our consciousness is a tool to help us get what we want.

How? Well, we already did it. We got clear about what we wanted. This act in and of itself, when revisited, has the power to remind our consciousness what it is we are working on: our dreams, our goals, and how to achieve them. This is important because opportunities are all around us. They're waiting for us to see them, to create them, and to recognize their value. Most of the time though, we're too caught up in our daily lives to notice. Getting clear with what we want and putting the *Finding My Dream* list in a place we see everyday is a way to guide that same awareness that changes matter just by being you. When we realize this, we tap into the infinite potential all around us and we stay aware, ready to take advantage of the next opportunity and the next.

Have you ever seen a car for the first time and then all of a sudden you see a ton of them? Or maybe your friend gets a pug dog and then all of a sudden, you can't stop seeing dogs everywhere? Chances are the dogs and cars were there already. Your awareness shifted and now you see them everywhere. The same happens with opportunities. They are always around, but our lack of awareness prevents us from seeing them. This awareness is what we created when we made our *Finding My Dream* list. In knowing what it is we are in the process of becoming, we stay open as opportunities present themselves.

A perfect example is this book. Last year, I came across a message on Instagram from a guy named Daniel Mignault asking to interview me on his podcast. I said yes, not knowing exactly what the interview was going to be about. We chatted about all sorts of stuff I was passionate about, including how I wanted to create a book to help others become the rock stars of their own lives. I didn't know Daniel was a published author himself! After the podcast, he told me he knew someone who could help get my book out to the world. The man's name is Jackson Dean Chase, and he is the editor of the words you're reading. He helped guide me into the world of writing and publishing. I could not have done it without him. And it all stemmed from knowing what I was working toward and saying yes to a fun but seemingly unrelated opportunity. If I wasn't clear with the Universe about getting my book out there, then I wouldn't have been introduced to the dude who helped make this book a reality! All because my awareness helped create my dream.

If we have the ability to change how matter behaves just by observing it, then we have the ability to program our mind to remake our reality into a world we choose. Which means you should:

- Flip what you want from negative to positive;

- Remind yourself who you are and what you want with your own personal affirmation list; and
- Remember what you wish to create in the future.

If you think of your life as a song, you're creating an epic masterpiece—a fist-pumping stadium anthem—and when you take to the stage, you won't be the only one singing it. Your friends and fans will be right there with you, cheering you on.

Questions to ask yourself:

- What do you want to create in your life? How is what you are thinking backing that up?
- Is your *Finding My Dream* list somewhere you can see everyday? Remember the power you have just by observing. Keep your list somewhere you see everyday helps remind the mind what you are creating.
- Are you open to opportunities as they are presented to you?

PART V

FEEL AND FLOW

Persistence is everything, and that means taking action. It could be massive, rapid action, or it could be slow, steady progress. Both can get you across the finish line, the only question is what kind of shape will you be in afterward? That's what we're going to focus on next, knowing your limits. Not the limits of your dream, but the limits of you: physically, mentally, emotionally, and spiritually. We're all human and can only do so much, so fast before burning out or injuring ourselves. It's important we take the time to talk about this now, before you rush off to take action.

That's why you need to know your limits—so you don't get hurt or fall apart on your quest to become the biggest, most badass version of yourself. It's all about balance. Let me give you another example, this time from a physical perspective: You're lifting weights at the gym and notice a shooting pain in your lower back. If you decide to keep lifting, it won't give you less pain, it will create more. It's your body's signal that something is wrong. I see this idea of fighting through our pain expressed so often in sports and business—that "on the other side of pain is success." I think that's crap. *On the other side of pain is more pain, not success!*

But that depends on the type of pain. We're talking about two types in this chapter, and knowing the difference can save your ass. The first is **warning pain**, the kind that sends a signal telling us to slow down, to be careful and reevaluate what we're doing and how we're doing it. Warning pains come in the style of throbbing aches or shooting pains. It's our body's way of saying, "Yo, chill out or find another way to do this." You know, before you get hurt.

This one time, I was practicing a really intense form of yoga. I was going at it hardcore, five or six times a week, often two classes back to back. I thought everything was going great, the more the better... until I developed a shooting pain at the bottom of my right butt cheek. The pain was bad enough to overcome my embarrassment, so I mentioned it to the instructor after class. She explained the area causing me pain was where my hamstring and butt muscles connected. She added that I might be on the verge of tearing my hamstring. I remember thinking, "What!? I practice yoga to have less pain, not more!" That was the wake up call I needed to shift how I practiced. What I was doing wasn't sustainable and my body was warning me to stop. I took the instructor's advice and laid low for a bit. When I got back to yoga, I began practicing a different style, one that I fell in love with and later became a certified yoga instructor of.

So that's the first type of pain, and if you get it, you need to stop what you're doing long enough to come up with a smarter way of doing it. If you don't, and you get injured or creatively burnt out, your dream is in trouble.

The second type of pain is **growing pain.** This is that

annoying, stubborn pain that prevents us from stepping into our true rock star self. It shows up when we're too scared to do something, or when we fear the result of getting what we want. So we let that fear of change hold us back. Sometimes, growing pains come in the form of excuses, doubts, or false beliefs; other times they come in the form of saying "I can't" and giving up. That's your ego blocking you from getting the results you want. That's the wall we're trying to move around or take down one brick at a time.

When we observe this pain, it's time to greet the challenge as an opportunity, a chance to progress, to keep going, keep persisting. What you are challenged by is here to make you better, more badass, and more epic—but only if you see it that way. If you choose to fall into victim mode, then you will continue to fall down the negative spiral. You don't need that. You deserve to feel good, be confident, and achieve your dreams.

Identify the pain you experience. Our bodies are smart and have different ways of communicating with us. Listen to what you're feeling; let your pain guide you. Question it and see if it is warning pain or growing pain.

Adjust if you feel warning pain. Allow your body to recharge, relax and restore. Self-care isn't selfish, and it allows us to accomplish more in the long-term. However, if you feel a growing pain come up, bring back the "Try Me" mindset we discussed earlier. Identify the obstacle as an opportunity to step up your game and perform like the rock star you are.

25

FINDING EASE AND THE POWER OF BREATH

I⟨T TOOK⟩ me a few years to realize how what I practiced reflected how I lived. Back in the day, I was practicing a very intense style of yoga that was more pose-based than movement-based. I didn't know the difference. I was just starting, so I needed to figure out what worked best for me.

In practicing this style, I realized my body looked amazing, I had tons of energy and felt great, but if I didn't get my hour-and-a-half sequence in each day, I'd get pissed off. I would be on tour angry at my band mates because I didn't get to practice my poses. Eventually, I realized that I was engaging in behavior that was the opposite of my goal.

My goal was to feel good and be able to find success in all areas of life, not in a cookie cutter kind of way, but in a way that helped me find my flow state regardless of the experience. The style I'd been practicing wasn't doing that for me.

Once I began experimenting with other styles of yoga, I realized just how ridiculous my expectations had been and how it's not about how much we do, it's about how often we show up. I learned that if yoga was all about posing then the most advanced yogis in the world would be in Cirque du Soleil or in the circus.

This was around the time I discovered a kind of yoga called Strala. Its founder, Tara Stiles, wrote the foreword to this book. I asked her because Strala Yoga changed my life. It's inspired from the ancient forms of *tai chi* and *qi gong*, along with principles of East Asian martial arts that place emphasis on moving rather than posing. The idea is we all have different bodies and move in different ways, making it important to discover what feels good to us as individuals.

Along with this idea of learning healthy ways to move was the idea we can do more by using less energy, which gives us more energy to do other things. This goes against the traditional mindset of having to work hard to get results. Instead of working harder, work smarter; it's possible to do more with less energy. Instead of nearly injuring myself like in past workouts, this philosophy guides others to move in ways that sustain a healthy lifestyle and find ease in the face of struggle.

So how do we practice this?

One way to do this is to soften. By that, I mean take a moment to notice if you are holding tension in your body. Are you flexing? Are you sitting or standing in a comfortable position? Just notice. Now, let go. Relax your shoulders. Let your head hang heavy. *Soften.* I know it sounds weird, but do it. Surrender. Let everything relax.

Surrender is how we create space. A lot of times, we hold on to stuff that doesn't serve us and that makes it tough to feel good and move comfortably. Imagine trying to move by flexing every muscle in your body. You would be stiff, and it would be tough. By relaxing and surrendering we let go of tension and free up the space to connect... But to connect with what?

To connect with our breath.

Our lungs are always moving. Even when we're completely still, our lungs are expanding and contracting. Our chest is rising and falling. Even when we're still, we're moving. In a way, this is a representation of flow. Softening creates space, letting go creates room to connect with the flow that's already happening within and bring it into our life.

From a relaxed position, I want you to breathe. Just breathe. Notice the breath coming in and out, how your chest expands, then contracts. You might find that your head naturally lifts with your shoulders on your inhale, and that you feel like you can let go even more as you exhale.

By practicing this for a few breaths, you tap into the flow that exists within you already. You don't need anything outside of yourself. You are enough right where you are. The act of softening and then breathing creates the relaxation response in your body. This helps you feel good and to find not only your flow state, but your inner peace and calm. The breath is one of the most calming tools we have. Using it from a place of surrender taps into your unlimited potential and helps you chill out in a quick and easy way. Try it. You can do it anywhere.

When you feel stressed or anxious, soften and breathe... See how you feel and remember, you have everything you need inside of you already.

Ultimate Relaxation Technique

If you're in a hurry or going through a tough time and need to chill out fast, here's my go-to technique. I do this before I go on stage if I'm feeling overwhelmed or overly excited. Try it with me while reading this. You can do it!

- Inhale nice and deep through your nose;
- Now exhale from your mouth as slow as you can;
- Make sure you exhale slower than you inhaled;
- Repeat at least three times, but continue however long you have time for.

The reason I love this technique is because it literally tells your heart to chill out. This act of exhaling slower than you inhale activates a connection between a nerve you have in your throat called the vagus nerve; this nerve has a direct relationship with your heart. By exhaling longer than you inhale, the vagus nerve sends a signal to our heart to slow down. By controlling our heart rate, it makes it easier to calm down and relax quickly.

You can use this ultimate relaxation technique anywhere and everywhere. Whip it out whenever you feel stressed or anxious. No one needs to know. Just inhale through your nose, then slowly exhale through your mouth. That's all it takes. Let it guide you through challenging times and see the results.

Square Breathing

Another one of the most powerful breathing techniques I've found to help calm the mind from anxiety and stress is what I refer to as "square breathing." It's easy and involves pauses between each inhale and exhale. In the pauses, some say we feel most alive. Creating the space between breaths allows a deeper opportunity to feel and to observe things like the sounds around us, the feelings within us, and the thoughts in our mind. Then we come back to our breath, giving time and space to observe both your internal world and your external world.

To do this:

- Inhale for a count of five; notice your breath filling your chest.
- Hold for a count of five.
- Exhale slowly for a count of five and feel the air being released from your body.
- Hold for another count of five and then repeat.

Practicing this technique helps create the space for us to observe our mind while creating the effortless flow state we referred to in earlier chapters. If you want to combine it with the ultimate relaxation technique, you can. All you have to do is exhale longer than you inhale.

Questions to ask yourself:

- How does what you practice reflect how you want to live?
- Are you holding tension in your body? Sometimes without even noticing?
- Can you relax, let go and breathe? If so, how does it feel?

26

MEDITATION: TAKE YOUR MIND ON A VACATION

WE ALL HAVE an image of what we think meditation is. Maybe it's a monk in the Himalayas wearing robes and chanting "Om," or maybe it's a person dressed in white, eyes closed, with a slight smile on their face. Whatever your view of meditation is, let it go. All the preconceived ideas, thoughts and mindsets that you have about meditation, let them go. I don't want your mind to be cloudy. So do your best to focus because I want to share with you another secret. One that has been right beneath your nose your entire life, and one that some don't learn until it's too late...

We touched on the power of breath in the last chapter, but now we're going to take it a step further. Are you ready? Take a deep breath in through your nose. When you can't breathe in anymore, exhale from your mouth as slow as you can.

Perfect! You did it. "Did what?" you may be asking. You just used one of the most powerful tools we have as human beings. *Meditation.* But what's so cool about it is you don't have to do anything different from what you're already doing. All you have to do is focus on your breath. Sounds easy, right? It is, but at the same time, it isn't. Where so many people go wrong is by thinking that meditation is a destination, a place we try to get to, like a beach vacation with our toes in the sand and waves in the background. The irony is meditation isn't a destination you can get to. The minute you think, "I'm meditating," you aren't.

From a mindfulness perspective, meditating is the act of coming back to the breath. Over and over. It means watching where your mind goes, then coming back to the breath. Noticing how you feel, then coming back to the breath. The process is the destination. You don't get there, *you are there*, and if you can breathe, you can meditate.

But why is it so powerful? Have you ever tried to see out of foggy or schmutzy glasses? That's the equivalent of our minds most of the time. Blurred out. Hard to focus. So when we come to our breath, simply observing each inhale and each exhale, we begin to clean our mental lens and see ourselves, others, and our experiences with a clarity we didn't have before.

Think of a two-liter bottle filled with water and sand. Imagine yourself shaking it up, then placing it on a table and watching the sand jump around inside the bottle. See it floating wildly, going every which way. That's like our mind. During the day, we get shaken up and our thoughts go everywhere. But as we practice coming to our breath, the shaking slows, and the pieces of sand float to the bottom, leaving clear, calm water above. That's what meditation is, its finding clarity, it's finding peace. We don't stay stuck in our thoughts, instead we observe them and allow them to settle by releasing our attachment to them.

When we meditate, we allow our minds to become clear like the water in the bottle. A clear mind creates new thoughts, new opportunities, new paths, and ways of thinking. A clear mind puts things in perspective; it allows us to watch our thoughts and recognize that obsessing over the past and stressing about the future doesn't serve us. Instead, we come to the most present thing we know, our breath. That is where we find our presence, that is where we find peace within ourselves.

Have you ever gone on vacation and your problems seemed less significant? Like you left them behind? Did your problems really change? No, your perspective did. And that's what's so awesome about meditation. It allows us to take our mind on vacation and create a new perspective right where we are. You don't have to fly to a tropical island or spend a bunch of money. In a sense, you bring the beach to you by focusing on your breath.

———

I CAN'T TELL you enough the importance of finding time to meditate everyday. The benefits are endless, and as we grow, meditation grants us the ability to find our balance and empower ourselves when things get hectic... because they will. Motivational speaker Jim Rohn said it best: "Don't wish for less problems, wish for more skills."

Meditation is a skill. One that can't be shown off because no one can experience what you experience—it all happens inside yourself.

There are many different kinds of meditation. What we've covered so far is a great foundation to begin your meditation practice: focus on your breath, notice what comes up, observe and then let go, come back to the breath. That's a great place to begin exploring. However, you may find yourself drawn to another meditation style or practice. If so, go with it and see how it feels. There's no one "right" way to do it, there's only the way that feels right for you.

For example, you might be told you have to sit up with your spine straight to meditate. Normally, I would agree that's helpful, but I also know sitting up isn't always possible. For me, this happens when I'm on the road and there's no place to sit, so I meditate lying down in my tour bus. It's about breathing, and you're always breathing. Consistency is more important than circumstance. You can meditate sitting up, lying down, or in any position you find safe, relaxing, and comfortable.

When I first attempted to meditate, I couldn't sit still. I constantly fidgeted and checked the clock, waiting for something mystical to happen. I didn't know if I was doing it right and was frustrated when I didn't see any results. This is normal. I often have people tell me they experience the same difficulties trying to meditate; they say stuff like, "I just can't sit still," or "It doesn't work for me."

If you have trouble calming down, don't try to calm down at all. Do something physical. From there, bringing focus to the breath helps access your flow state.

Make time to meditate each day. It could be in the morning or at night. Consistently showing up to do it is how you forge new habits. Dedicate this time for yourself. Meditation is one of the most powerful tools you have; it legit helps with everything. No joke! But don't take my word for it. Experience it yourself.

I challenge you to commit to meditating every day for the next week. Try to do it the same time every day. Any time is a good time, but many people find the best to be mornings (right after waking) or night time (right before bed).

Look at this experience as an experiment. See what

happens: how you feel, what goes through your mind. Just breathe. At its most basic level, that's all there is to it. Keep coming back to the breath. Let your mind wander, don't try to control it, just observe it, and come back to the breath. Remember, you don't have to be anywhere besides where you are right now. So if it's busy or somewhere you don't think you can meditate, I challenge you to try! It's always nice to meditate in the comfort of your home, or surrounded by nature, but that's not always possible. Meet the challenge as an opportunity to show up and practice.

When I was leading yoga classes on the Warped Tour where I met Gene Simmons, I often dealt with loud generators, high traffic areas, and sometimes, even metal bands playing around us. I told everyone in my class, "If you can meditate here, you can meditate anywhere!" And you know what? We did.

Don't let your environment dictate your peace of mind. Use any annoying external sounds to take yourself deeper into your flow. The trick for occasional disruptive noise is to observe it like you observe your thoughts and come back to your breath. Let it go. You are not your environment, you are the creator of your environment. Observing it allows for that level of awareness to flow into your mind. Surrendering is how we deepen our practice in hectic situations. Just breathe.

Questions to ask yourself:

- Can you incorporate focused breathing into a physical exercise that you already do? See how conscious breathing impacts your physical activity.

- Do you feel like your mind is jumping all over the place? That's okay. Let it go, practice coming back to your breath.
- Are you willing to start a meditation practice? Commit to once a day for a week. Try three minutes in the morning or at night. Make a goal to do it everyday for that week and write down your experience.

27

STANDING IN THE FACE OF NEGATIVITY

WHEN OBSERVING your thoughts during meditation, you might find a lot of negativity coming up. This is normal, and it's why a lot of people give up. They're afraid to look too deeply into their own darkness. This darkness could take the shape of negative thoughts or beliefs about yourself or others. It can be disturbing to suddenly become aware of them and how much they affect your life. Once you're aware of the problems they cause, you get the opportunity to confront and replace them with positive thoughts and beliefs. This could be through meditation, affirmations, yoga, hypnosis, or therapy, and in whatever combination feels right. We've gone over some of those already, and hypnosis and therapy go beyond the scope of this book. What I want to suggest then is another quick and easy technique to stay positive when you're surrounded by negativity. It's one I've found helpful and use all the time.

In order to maintain our energy, we need to make sure we learn how to increase it. That's why I'm going to share with you my favorite way to increase energy fast!

Exercise: Uplifting Yourself

There are two parts to this exercise. The first is stepping into an attitude of gratitude. It's not always easy, but there's always something we can be grateful for. When we feel our energy sinking or like we're getting roughed up by life, come back to what you are grateful for. Think about the things in your life you can express gratitude for having. Maybe it's the ability to see, or hear. Maybe it's the people in your life—the relationships. Or maybe it's your heart, your mind, or body, or perhaps the clothes on your back. Whatever it is, express gratitude by saying thank you. Things like anger, fear, and resentment don't exist with a grateful spirit. So uplift yourself with the "attitude of gratitude" and be thankful for the little things.

It's easy to forget how blessed we are. Someone, somewhere would love to be you. Think about that. Really think. Understand how powerful that statement is, and how powerful you are because of it. Be grateful for what you have, and for the drive to get what you want out of life. That's the rock star way.

For the second part of this exercise, I want you to put one hand on your belly, and take slow, deep breaths. While you breathe in, expand your chest and try to push your belly out into your hand. If pushing is hard for you, just focus on the feeling of having your chest expand. As you exhale, focus on trying to soften and relax. Let your shoulders chill out; relax your head, face, and neck. You can have your eyes open or closed. If they're open, notice what's around you: the sounds, the colors. If your eyes are closed, focus on the sensations of your body: your clothes, your breath, your hand touching your belly.

With this technique, you are connecting to your inner

and outer environment. Through the combination of intentional breathing and awareness of what's around us (the colors, the sounds, the feelings), we increase our energy. It's like seeing others as having a million followers, except now we're seeing the entire world that way, with the same energy, including ourselves. Seen this way, we're all brilliant, beautiful, and abundant.

This helps us recharge our energy. Because the energy is always around us. We just have to bring our attention to it and breathe it in.

Use this belly breathing technique to increase your energy whenever you feel low or depleted. If you're in public and don't want to put your hand on your belly, you don't have to. Just breathe. Look for the beauty and value that's around you. *Appreciate it.* See if you notice anything changing... Colors might seem more vibrant, or you might notice things you never did before.

Test it. See what happens.

Questions to ask yourself:

- Are you willing to look at your negative thoughts and beliefs in order to transform them? It might feel awkward but you can do it.
- What people or areas of your life tend to drain you of your energy? Uplift yourself with the exercise we just did if you start to feel drained.
- Do you know how blessed you are? Take a minute to count ten things you're grateful for. Start with things about yourself, then move to other areas of your life like your family, friends, and other things.

28

CREATING LASTING CHANGE

You've come so far. I'm proud of you. Most people don't make it this far. Since you're still here, that tells me you're dedicated to your own personal transformation. That takes commitment. You are a true rock star!

So how do we continue to create the lasting change you need, to not only live your dream but to keep it? To start, use this book as a reference any time you feel stuck or need a quick burst of positive energy. Creating lasting change doesn't happen overnight, it comes from showing up day after day to learn, to grow, and keep getting better. That doesn't mean you'll feel great every day. It doesn't mean you'll have all the answers or make the right decisions. You don't have to. You just have to keep going. You'll grow into who you need to be as you go, like a butterfly emerging from a cocoon. That's a beautiful thing. But without taking action, you'll stay right where you are. So remember why you do what you do. Remember the greater purpose you are here to serve. Remember the people you stand for—those who become greater because you become greater.

Creating a new habit takes time. For most, that's about

two months. But we're not trying to just create habits, we're creating a lifestyle, a total transformation in how we think. This affects everything you do, and allows you to meet obstacles as opportunities. It allows you to step into your power with love and compassion for others. Not asking "Why me?" but stating "Try me!" Stay true to your process. Like meditation, it's all about showing up over and over again being willing to step into the life you are creating.

Questions to ask yourself:

- In what ways will you keep taking action to creating lasting change? Write down three things you plan to do to keep the positive momentum rolling.
- How can you shift from a "Why me?" mentality to a "Try me!" mentality and keep it that way?
- What do you stand for? What is your purpose?

29

FINAL CHAPTER

As we come to the end of the book, I want you to understand how powerful you are. The whole reason for creating this book is to empower you, to guide you in bringing out the rock star that lies within. You don't need anyone to tell you how to live, or if you're doing it right or wrong. You're the rock star of your life, the only one capable of taking charge and stepping into your triumph.

Let your life be an example of what you are capable of. Know that in the face of self doubt, anxiety, and fear, you stand strong... Sometimes shaking, sometimes unsure, and sometimes afraid, but you still stood, and you continue to stand and pursue your dream. You do it because you know what you want, you know what to do. That drive is already within you. It always has been, waiting for you to step on stage and take charge. You must keep going, one step at a time.

I want you to remember the positive affirmation list you created at the beginning of this book. Hopefully, you hung it up somewhere you can see it all the time. If you ever feel like you're in a negative space, in need of clarity, or just want to feel good, revisit your list and take some small action. The action is where the magic happens. The world will move with you if you move too, but *you must take action*.

For the times when you doubt yourself, because you will, know a breakthrough is coming. Choose love over fear.

Your circumstance does not define you. Only you define YOU, and even then, you have potential beyond your comprehension. So never stop learning, never stop growing, and always listen to understand rather than to react.

Treat others the way you wish to be treated. Make relationships your priority, not things, and you will set yourself free from the limits the world might try to impose on you.

And finally, remember you are never alone. You are always right where you're supposed to be. Come back to this book if you feel lost or in need of a reminder of how epic you are.

Thank you for showing up.

Thank you for being you.

You are the rock star.

NOTES

USE THESE PAGES FOR YOUR THOUGHTS AND IDEAS.

_____
_____
_____
_____
_____
_____
_____
_____
_____
_____
_____
_____
_____
_____
_____
_____
_____
_____

RESOURCES

For more content, please visit **YouAreTheRockStar.com**

If you're interested in learning more about yoga and what it can do for you, I've written a quick, fun guide for beginners called *Foundational Flow: The Beginner's Yoga Guide* that helps ease you into your practice. It's available in ebook and paperback.

If you'd like to enjoy the same style of yoga I do, please visit my friend, Tara Stiles, at her site: https://stralayoga.com/

For more positive affirmations, check out Justin Perry's YouAreCreators channel on YouTube, in particular: "How to Be a Money Magnet"

READING LIST

- *Autobiography of a Yogi* by Paramahansa Yogananda
- *Buddhist Bootcamp* by Timber Hawkeye
- *The Celestine Prophecy* by James Redfield
- *The Four Agreements* by Don Miguel Ruiz
- *The Law Of Attraction* by Michael J. Losier
- *Make Your Bed* by William H. McRaven
- *The Music Lesson* by Victor Wooten
- *No Matter What!* by Lisa Nichols
- *The Secret* by Rhonda Byrne
- *The Seven Habits Of Highly Effective People* by Steven Covey
- *Siddhartha* by Herman Hesse
- *The Subtle Art Of Not Giving a F*ck* by Mark Manson
- *The Surrender Experiment* by Michael Alan Singer
- *Think & Grow Rich* by Napoleon Hill
- *The Traveler's Gift* by Andy Andrews
- *You Are a Badass* by Jen Sincero

ACKNOWLEDGMENTS

Special Thanks:

Jackson Dean Chase, Ralph Woodrow, Nancy Woodrow, John Woodrow, Joyce Woodrow, Taylor Woodrow Corriveau, Kenzie Woodrow, Tristan Corriveau, Dallis Seeker, Kaya Reagan, Sheila McNamee, Ricky Carvalho, Alex Pratt, Victoria Alvanos, Beth Crawford, Catie Macken, J.C. Lippold, Tara Stiles, Mike Taylor, Lisa Nichols, Stacey Plummer, Lin Illingworth, and Becky Balfour.

The entire Woodrow family, Nana, The Bourgoin Family, The Esposito Family, and The Leonard Family.

Deepa Mehta, Louis Fisher, Sunny Dilinger, Kevin Paris, Blu, Amir Magal, Dean Zeller, and everyone in my tribe.

Nancy Wentworth, Matt Wentworth, Trevor Wentworth, Timothy Molloy, Richard Dyke, Rich Johnston, Joel Tyrrell, Jenna McDougall, Jeff Yeager, David Rassmussen, Tyler Calkin, John Young, Lucas Starr, Kyle and Micah Hogarth.

Dylan Martinusen, Sara Salkins, Shannon McCoy, Valérie Bodry, Chelsey Dirn, Rhyan Gaspari, Guendanabani Castro, Martina Wágnerová, Nel Nuytkens, Terezie Lagová, Veronika Gschwandtner, Roxsana Roca, Marla Tomlinson,

Tanya Tischendorf, Christina Burgos, Irene Egea Pérez, Jasmin Ketschler, Katerina Doležalova, Alexander Almafi, Pauline Pfeil, Kristina Osipovich, Jules Franz, Dara Torres, Marie-Andrée Gilbert, Ashley M. Plumley, and everyone who has had a positive impact in my life. I wouldn't be who I am without you being who you are. Thank you for being you, and thank you for your reflection.

ABOUT THE AUTHOR

Alexander "Woody" Woodrow is a founding member of the rock band Our Last Night, one of the largest independent bands in the world with over two million fans. He believes we are here to be of service and to give others the tools to rock at life. He currently lives in Nashville, TN.

For more content, please visit
YouAreTheRockStar.com

 facebook.com/woodywoodrowyoga

 twitter.com/WoodyOLN

 instagram.com/woodywoodrow